PRENTICE-HALL
FOUNDATIONS OF CATHOLIC THEOLOGY SERIES

FOUNDATIONS OF CATHOLIC THEOLOGY SERIES

Gerard S. Sloyan, *Editor*

THE
THREE PERSONS
IN ONE GOD

GERARD S. SLOYAN

The Catholic University of America
Washington, D.C.

PRENTICE-HALL, INC.
Englewood Cliffs, N.J.

Nihil obstat:

Charles J. Ring, CPS, SSL
Censor Deputatus

Imprimatur:

✠ Patrick A. O'Boyle, DD
Archbishop of Washington

October 8, 1963

The *nihil obstat* and *imprimatur* are official
declarations that a book or pamphlet is free
of doctrinal or moral error. No implication is
contained therein that those who have granted
the *nihil obstat* and *imprimatur* agree with
the content, opinions, or statements expressed.

PRENTICE-HALL INTERNATIONAL, INC., *London*
PRENTICE-HALL OF AUSTRALIA, PTY., LTD., *Sydney*
PRENTICE-HALL OF CANADA, LTD., *Toronto*
PRENTICE-HALL FRANCE S.A.R.L., *Paris*
PRENTICE-HALL OF INDIA PRIVATE LIMITED, *New Delhi*
PRENTICE-HALL OF JAPAN, INC., *Tokyo*
PRENTICE-HALL DE MEXICO, S.A., *Mexico City*

C

54112

EDITOR'S NOTE

This series offers the depth and richness of the divine message of salvation proclaimed to us by Christ. The theology, or "faith seeking understanding," contained here is not on a catechetical level, nor yet on a complex, higher level; it is clear and nontechnical, but at the same time adult and thorough. It is a scholarly presentation of revelation.

These volumes do not adopt an apologetic approach. They neither attempt to justify Catholic faith nor aim at convincing those who do not profess it of the reasonableness of believing. This series is written primarily for those who already believe, who accept the Church as the living continuation of Christ, and the Scriptures as divinely inspired.

The authors do not attempt a philosophy of God or of Christianity, but a study of the mystery of God seen through the eyes of faith. The mystery of faith will not be dispelled by the study of these books. It will remain.

Since some background in philosophy on the part of the reader is needed, and cannot in every case be presumed, there are times when philosophical terms will need to be explained. Philosophical reasoning is very much a part of speculative theology.

Although the breakdown of the series is along traditional lines, each volume is designed to emphasize the oneness of God's plan of salvation and not its different facets. Distinction is made in order to unite. What is taught in the Scriptures is stressed, so that it may be seen how men of the Bible understood the message entrusted to them. The historical aspects of doctrine as held by Christians are then treated: the testimony of the early Christian writers and the liturgy to the belief of the Church; the controversies and heresies that necessitated defense and precise formulation, and finally, the magisterial teaching in each subject area. In this way speculative theology, or the present understanding of each mystery, is not seen in isolation from the sources of faith.

Thus, the revealed Christian message is viewed as the *tradition* (in the fullest and best sense of that theological term) expressed in and through the Church over the centuries—more explicitly formulated, from age to age, and with further applications. But it is still the same saving message begun in the Old Testament and perfected in the mystery and person of Jesus Christ.

One last point is important. Although the study of theology is an exercise of intellect, it can never be exclusively this. The message of Jesus Christ is a living Word, an invitation to participate in the saving event of the redemption, starting in this world by faith and the union of grace, and culminating in heaven by vision and immediate union. This invitation demands response or living faith. The study of the Christian message through theology requires such response, for the message is not something that was heard and assented to once. It is a Word addressed to us that requires our vigorous "Yes" for a lifetime.

CONTENTS

vii

CHAPTER TWO

THE EXTRA-BIBLICAL WITNESS OF THE FIRST THREE CENTURIES, *page 29*

CHAPTER THREE

THE ARIAN CRISIS AND AFTER, *page 53*

CHAPTER FOUR

FROM AUGUSTINE TO THE COUNCILS OF REUNION, *page 81*

Trinitarian piety, the fruit of anti-Arianism. From Boethius to the dialecticians. Peter the Lombard. St. Thomas Aquinas. The question of the filioque. The relation of mission to procession.

CHAPTER FIVE

THE INDWELLING OF THE DIVINE THREE, *page 101*

SELECTED READINGS, *page 109*

ABBREVIATIONS, *page 111*

INDEX, *page 113*

"The blessed Abraham saw the Trinity, as far as man can, and regaled It as a good friend." "The holy Abraham regales of old the Godhead, who is one in three Persons." (Cf. Gn 18) (Russian icon of the Holy Trinity; courtesy UNESCO; reproduced from *UNESCO Album, USSR*)

INTRODUCTION

It is impossible to overemphasize the importance of the Christian doctrine that God is one in three persons. This has correctly been called the teaching distinctive of the Christian faith, that which sets the approach of Christians to the "fearful mystery" of the deity apart from all other approaches. To be human is to be separated from God in some degree. To be Christian, the Christian believes, is to be separated from him least.

It is true that the person of Jesus Christ is central, not peripheral, to Christianity. He is central, however, not as the end-term of the creature's activity but as the revealer of the secrets of the Infinite which he both is and is not, being God and man. It is Jesus Christ both as eternal Word uttered in the inmost recesses of the being of God and as glorified Lord and Christ at the Father's right hand whom Christians worship; but to say that is not to say all that must be said of him.

The ultimate meaning of Jesus Christ is that in his manhood he makes known to us men the God of whom it is truer to say that he is unknown than that he is known. First Jesus reveals his Father to us through all that the Father does to save us in him, the Son. Then he reveals the Spirit, whom he sends from the Father. In the fullest measure that God is known to men he is known as Three who are distinct yet One. This knowledge of God has been achieved through Jesus Christ. He has lessened human separation or "apartness" from the Infinite.

The importance of the teaching that God is One in Three is evident if we examine the nature of religion. All religion is a struggle of the human spirit to be at one with the One. If in Jesus Christ the true nature of the One has been revealed, and if the One invites man to be one with him through this same Jesus, then a deeper union is possible because it is based on the real knowledge that comes with disclosure. To those who do not know him by means of this disclosure, close union remains impossible; there can be only striving.

Mysticism has been defined as "the secret knowledge of God." Intimacy is the hallmark of all love, and of mystical love in particular. There can be love only to the degree that there is mutual knowledge in the lovers. If the essence of God is that the great Alone is in some mysterious way Three who engage in an unending intercommunion of love, the creature aware of this inner dynamic is in a favored condition indeed. He is open to the possibility of being drawn into the life of the One—who is Three—in a way no others are. He can experience a personal relation to each of the Three—a relation unavailable to those who do not possess this knowledge. The man who knows the One only as One, knows him but imperfectly. In a certain real sense he knows him falsely, for God as Three is not only richer and fuller but indeed *other* than this man supposes him to be.

It would be foolish and harmful, however, to boast that the God of the Christians is the God who is, whereas the God of Judaism and of

Islam is the God who is not. Already there are factors enough to draw believers in the one God away from each other; no more are needed. The great common ground of those we term "monotheists" is that they know God as uncreated, as eternal, as limitless in every way. For him, distinctness from the universe is not a limitation but a perfection. The creation, being finite, is at base a potential largely unfulfilled. The Absolute of the monotheist is totally self-realized, personal. Personality for him is not a limitation of being (as it partly is with angels and men) but is the zenith of being. An Absolute which cannot say "I am" is less than the child who can; the sum total of billions who can say "I am" constitutes, conversely, no Absolute. Only the God revealed to us through Moses and all the prophets is such a one, the God who is Father of our Lord Jesus Christ, revealed to us in the Spirit. The God whom Muhammad knew from Christian and Jewish traditions and from his pious reflections on the traditions of his desert ancestors is this one true God. Indeed, he is All, and there is no other than he.

It is in this awareness of God, we have said, that monotheism's great common hope lies. To know God as do large segments of the non-Christian East is to know him as the soul of the universe, as inextricable from it. He is ubiquitous spirit, the All in all. All that is is he and he is All that is. Yet what certain Eastern traditions call "limitless" in the deity monotheism finds circumscribed, unless each is misunderstanding the other badly. It would be reassuring to both the East and West, Christian and non-Christian alike, if there were enough common elements in their respective mystical traditions to give promise of future unity of religious striving. Too often it comes to light that despite certain identical elements in the experience of the Absolute, there are grave, even essential, differences of view concerning the Absolute experienced.

Jew, Muslim, and Christian do not begin with any handicap of confusing God with his world. Yet both Jew and Muslim hold it against the Christian that he is badly confused on the nature of the deity. God is One or he is no God, say these two traditions, Judaism the parent and Islam the near kinsman of Christianity. The Christian faith has committed the unpardonable sin in their eyes of introducing plurality into the deity. Worse still, in its "mystery of the incarnation" Christianity has put a man on the plane of God, a confusion bordering on blasphemy.

The Christian does not fully comprehend his faith until he is clear on the meaning of these two major charges against it and can show them to be unfounded. He has not grasped his own belief fully until he can propose faith in a tripersonal God as a richer and truer conception of the One; he must present him not as less one but as unique and supremely unitary in being Father, Son, and Spirit. Having established that mathematical discreteness has nothing to do with these Three (the number "three" being used analogously and not in its quantitative sense, even though the orthodox Fathers of the Church insisted on the phrase "Three in number" [en arithmōi], to make clear that the persons were absolutely distinct and unconfused), the Christian must go on to show that the introduction of the circumscribed, human Jesus is not the piece of inexpert myth-making it may seem to others. He must know that the idea of "a god in human form" does not neutralize forever any sublimer conception of the Absolute. It must be stressed that the human nature of Jesus, being a creature, is incapable of acquiring the essence of deity, and that the union of the Word with this nature unto eternity is not a scaling down of the Boundless to human dimensions.

In a word, the mystery of the three persons in one God must be seen primarily as a mystery of his incomprehensibility. It is in no sense an affair of a tidy trio of partners or some tricephalous beast whose inherent absurdity religious faith is able to disregard.

Secondly, those of other religious persuasions than the Christian must be helped to see that while delighting in their own union with the Absolute and dismissing caricatures such as Grant Wood's "New England Gothic" or Ogden Nash's "purple papal people," they may not so easily be rid of the God of the Christians. Neither may they dismiss the holy assembly (ekklēsía) that invokes him and is a sacrament of him as incurably institutionalized and middle-class. As much union with the All as they could possibly seek he has first invited them to, out of his unsounded trinitarian depths.

Lastly, the Christian himself must know the Father, the Son, and the Spirit at a level of intimacy or his "faith" is not faith but a conundrum to him. The New Testament writings hymn the unity and distinctness of the Three; the creeds make it explicit; the liturgy is freighted with it. The invitation of Christ is extended to those who will admit the Three within their beings: "We will come to him and make our abode with him."

Heavenly existence is nothing if not a participation in the life of the
4 Three, just as Christian existence is the same participation experienced

beforetime in lesser degree. Eternal life is to know the Father and the only Son whom he has sent, in the Spirit.

This is Christianity as well—assuming that the knowledge will show the Christian faithful in deeds of love.

All else is commentary.

"The angel answered, The Holy Spirit will come upon you, and the power of the Most High will overshadow you; and for that reason the holy child to be born will be called 'Son of God.'" (Lk 1, 35) (*Annunciation* by an anonymous artist; courtesy National Gallery of Art, Washington, D.C.; Rosenwald Collection)

CHAPTER ONE

THE REVELATION
OF THE MYSTERY
IN HOLY SCRIPTURE

It is a matter beyond all question that there was no knowledge of the Trinity in the Old Testament period. This came only with the person and message of Jesus Christ. True, the early Christian Fathers found references to the mystery implicit throughout the Hebrew Scriptures, but this was because of the vantage point of their developed faith. The sages of Israel came to no such conclusion, and among these there were

7

many who pored over the sacred books with a perfect love and devotion. The favored texts of the patristic period in this regard included those which described the Lord taking counsel with himself during the work of creation and afterwards (Gn 1,26; 3,22; 11,7); the appearance of the three individuals at Abraham's tent (Gn 18,2); the hymn of the Thrice-Holy (*triságion*) sung by seraphs in the vision of Isaia (6,2ff) which has become the *Sanctus* of the Mass in the Western rites. Greater familiarity with Oriental speech patterns discloses, however, both the "plural of majesty" and the repetition of the number three for emphasis, which together account for these usages.

ANGEL, SPIRIT, WORD, WISDOM IN THE OLD TESTAMENT

Another set of provocative texts consists of those which feature the "angel of Yahweh" who deals with persons and objects in place of the Lord himself. (Gn 16,7; 32,31; Ex 3,2) He has divine status, but on examination proves to be in no way distinct from the Lord. This is merely a verbal convention from the later period of biblical composition to suggest that an intermediary more fittingly deals with the creation than the Lord himself. This idea developed gradually. In the eighth- and seventh-century period of the prophets it both appears and recedes. By the post-exilic fifth century Yahweh's transcendence over nature is a firmly fixed conception. He no longer deals with creation directly, as he had done in the more robust speech of the earlier period. Philo, the Jewish theologian of Alexandria (d. ca. 45 A.D.) tended to see in this "messenger of Yahweh" an intermediary, while Christian writers interpreted the term as a manifestation of the Word out of due time. It is doubtful that the usage has any significance whatever as trinitarian revelation in the strict sense.

The Old Testament terms "spirit," "word," and "wisdom" which are of frequent occurrence also received ample commentary at Christian hands. The former two came to denominate the third and second persons in God respectively, and the latter term "wisdom" both persons, though more usually the Son. Hippolytus and Tertullian provided the exceptions to this, but their designation of the Holy Spirit as "wisdom" did not

prevail.

God's Spirit

Spirit (Heb. *ruah*) meant the breath of life to the ancient Israelite. Hence Yahweh, whose distinctive feature was that he lived, uniquely, and caused life, received the name Spirit. When the term did not signify lifebreath it meant the mighty power of the wind, whether destructive (Ps 28[29],8f; 1 Kgs 19,11ff) or creative: "By the word of the Lord the heavens were made, and all their host by the breath of his mouth." (Ps 32[33],6; cf. Ez 37,9f.) In one poignant passage above cited (1 Kgs 19,12), the Lord sighs like a gentle breeze. (Cf. Jn 3,8.) The "spirit of the Lord" is frequently employed as a phrase for the Lord himself, though at times this spirit seems to be objectified as if it were more than merely a way to describe the one God. Thus, when the Lord sends his spirit upon Saul (1 Sam 10,6), upon his servant from Jesse's stem (Is 11,2), or on the people Israel (Jl 2,28f), it is quite understandable why Christians who now knew the Spirit as a person should have discovered him in this graphic wording of Scripture.

The essence of the prophetic gift in Israel came to be the descent of the "spirit of Yahweh" on someone. (Ez 2,2) Hence it is not surprising that in the early Christian centuries the Holy Spirit was defined simply in terms of this function, by way of verbal coincidence: "He through whom the prophets spoke of old." The pious Israelite was one whose spirit was open to God's spirit. (Pss 50[51],12; 103[104],30) It was widely supposed that in the days of the Messia God's spirit would be poured out upon his people, slave and freeman alike (Is 32,15; Ez 11,19), in full measure, and upon the central messianic figure in a special way. (Cf. Is 11,2; 42,1.)

It is evident from these and other Old Testament texts that the Lord of Israel was thought of as communicating with men "by" or "in" his spirit; but that this spirit was conceived of as having a separate personal existence from the Lord himself there is no biblical evidence. The Lord *is* spirit, being the source of all life and movement. Other than he there is no one who is, or who is spirit. All the gods of the gentiles are demons.

God's Word

Because anthropomorphic representations of the Lord gave the early Hebrew writers no pause whatever, we are not surprised to find that he who "breathes" supremely is also the utterer of a "word." His word, like his breath, both creates and sets in order. (Ps 32[33],6; cf. Gn 1,2.) Perhaps the best known of Old Testament texts concerned with the Lord's creative word—surely the most poetic—speaks of the holy results he expects of his life-giving word: "As the rain and the snow drop down from the heavens and do not return without watering the earth and making it fruitful . . . giving seed to the sower and bread to the eater, so it is with the word that comes forth from my mouth; it does not return to me inefficacious; it achieves what I will it to, it fulfills its mission." (Is 55,10f)

The Lord's word in Old Testament Scripture (or better, his "utterance") is always twofold: it is fulfilled first in the visible creation, which springs into existence as a result of it; its second and finer fulfillment is Torah, that "word of instruction" uttered out of love which sets the pious Israelite heart in harmony with the Lord who speaks to it. (Dt 28,58; 30,10–14; Ps 118[119]) The later rabbis would even claim that Torah preexisted the framing of the universe.

There is admittedly in this twofold usage a perfect preparation for the use of "the word of the Lord" to designate a person, but there is no indication that the biblical writers so employed it. Later writers like Philo and even the inspired author of the Book of Wisdom (ca. 90 B.C.) come close to personalizing the "word" and "wisdom" of earlier biblical books, but deeper scrutiny reveals that these usages are no more than poetic figures to describe Yahweh himself. As one who communicates with men and is the begetter of all holiness, Yahweh both speaks and shares the wisdom he possesses uniquely.

God's Wisdom

Wisdom, like word and spirit, is either a property of the divine or the very deity himself. In no sense is it another than he. One does not find wisdom abroad on the earth or even in the deep. It is with the Lord. By it he measures the waters, instructs the winds, gives laws for the rain and the sunlight. (Jb 28,12–28) Wisdom is mistress of her own house who sets a feast of the mind. (Prv 9,1–6) She precedes all his glorious works (Prv 8,22ff); in fact he does them through her. She pre-exists all creation, simply because he does. (Sir 24,3ff) From being his eternal companion she becomes Israel's companion. Even when the Stoic-influenced Alexandrian author of the Book of Wisdom calls her "the aura of the might of God and a pure effusion of the glory of the Al-mighty" (Wis 7,25f), he stops short of personifying her. For the Israelite —whatever philosophical and cultural influences he may have undergone —there was no one but the One. It was Yahweh's very richness that cried out for a vocabulary which hinted at alternation of some sort, he to whom all that he had made stood in a relation of "other."

There is no true personification of the Lord's attributes in all the canonical wisdom literature taken together. When the Christian author of the Epistle to the Hebrews later comes to apply wisdom texts to the eternal Word, however, he has the needed phrasing ready to hand. (Heb 1,2.3; 4,12) [1] Without the revelation of the relation of the Word to the Father, made in Jesus Christ, the author of Hebrews would have been no farther along than his Jewish rabbinic contemporaries.

PERSONIFICATION IN INTERTESTAMENTAL LITERATURE

This brief discussion of preparation for the mystery of the Trinity within the Israelite milieu would not be complete unless it spoke of the Jewish writings composed between the two collections of inspired Scrip-ture or during the New Testament period. Spirit, word, and wisdom clearly stood for manifestations of God's creative and sanctifying power in the Old Testament, but in books like the *Testament of the Twelve Patriarchs,* the first or Ethiopian *Book of Henoch,* or the *Parables [Simili-tudes] of Henoch* (chs. 37–69 of the latter), they reached an apogee of "personification." There was, in first place, great emphasis in these writ-ings on a host of spirits, good and bad, either doing God's will or resisting it. These intermediaries between God and his world were perhaps sub-stitutes in the popular mind for the prophets, of whom none had ap-peared since the exile. The heavens seemed shut up against the longings of Hebrew hearts. In consequence Yahweh was "Lord of the Spirits" when he was not the *Shekinah* ("Presence, Glory") or *Memra* ("Word,"

[1] A period between verse numbers indicates that the verses cited are successive but nonconsecutive.

in Aramaic—seemingly a verbal tessera to avoid pronunciation of the divine name). At all points these titles *could* bear the meaning—though they were in no sense intolerant of any other—of someone distinct from the Lord. When there were no prophets or spokesmen in the strict sense, an alternate scheme of mediation was almost bound to assert itself. In fact, it did so in these late Jewish writings.

The high point it reached was in descriptions of the Lord's *Messia*, his anointed king through whom he would establish a kingdom of holiness ushering in the "last days." This chosen individual was to be a man, undoubtedly. The Jews never entertained any notion but that. So intimate was to be his relation to Yahweh, however, that any attribute proper to God might with equal fittingness be applied to him. Isaia (7,13f) and Michea (5,2) speak of a Davidic figure in general terms, but the second-century author of Daniel makes his role specific. (7,13f) For the author of Psalm 109[110] he is great King David's "master."

Once we get outside the canonical collection, the titles and prerogatives of this mysterious personage flourish. We know "Emmanuel" ("God with us") from the Isaian prophecy (Is 7,14) understood in its fullest possible sense. The non-canonical *Psalms of Solomon* (ca. 100–60 B.C.) says that all nations will tremble before him in fear, and his power shall be his trust in the Lord. Sinless, he shall destroy sinners by the word of his mouth; God shall make him powerful by his holy spirit, and wise, and unequivocally just. (17,40) He shall lead his people to good pastures, this king of majesty whom the Lord will raise up to give direction to Israel's paths. The encomiums are even greater in the *Parables of Henoch* (170 B.C.?–100 A.D.?). There he is a "son of man" who is the intimate of the Lord of Spirits, the "Ancient of Days." Holiness dwells with him. No secrets of the Lord are kept from him, and he will reveal them when he comes to "smash the teeth of sinners and overturn kings, destroying their thrones and their power." (46,4) The Lord of Spirits chose him, "knew his name," before the creation of the sun and all the stars; this elect one will be like a staff for the pious desert folk to lean on, their light and their hope. (48,3ff)

All of these claims and titles are the more comprehensible when we consider the fact of the fall of Jerusalem to the conquering Romans under Pompey (63 B.C.). The Jews were without human hope; therefore their trust in the Lord was doubly intensified. More than that, their inspired Book of Daniel, so clearly in the apocalyptic *genre*, served as the archetype for any number of similar apocalypses. The vision of "one like a son of man" in Daniel 7 was repeated with endless variations and exaggerations. The messianic figure these writings yielded, while human, was above angels and men because he was to judge them both; he pre-existed creation in some way, and is intimately under the protection of Yahweh with whom he will rule in the final age. The Palestinian Targum, or paraphrase of the Scriptures in triumphant Aramaic, went so far as to expunge the notion of suffering completely from the Servant Poems of the Second Isaia, especially ch. 53, by rendering them in the opposite sense to the effect that sinners would suffer in his day, not that he would suffer.

THE LOGOS
AS INTERMEDIARY IN PHILO

Many obscurities attend the picture of the language of mediation in late Jewish sources, but in its main lines it is as stated above. It is no cause for surprise, therefore, that the Alexandrian Jewish writer Philo should have attempted to harmonize the Middle Platonic idea of God (first centuries B.C. and A.D.) as Supreme Mind and Supreme Good with the transcendent Lord of Israel; the "powers" of Platonic thought with the Lord's operations as abstractions apart from himself; and the Logos, that is, world of forms or archetypes of the visible creation (in the Stoic system *lógos* = reason or plan), with the chief intermediary between God and the universe. Philo's Logos is not easy to identify. Knowing from his Greek Bible that the Lord had created all things "by his *lógos*," and likewise that he had revealed himself to the prophets by his word, Philo tended to see in the Logos both God's agent in creation and the medium by which the human mind gets in touch with him.

It should be made clear that in no sense was this older contemporary of Jesus less than fully Jewish. All Philo's contacts with the Greek philosophic schools of his native Alexandria were used by him to make the pagans see the truth and reasonableness of Israel's revelation, the Pentateuch especially. He is very strong on the unity of God, so much so that it would be a mistake to think that his Logos doctrine weakened his Jewish convictions on this point in any way. Whenever he speaks of God or his works, he does so in a detached philosophical vocabulary quite unlike the Bible with its warmth of poetic expression. Because *13* Philo conceived God as unknowable, inexpressible, and transcendent (*apoíos*—i.e., without quality, above species and genus), he had to bring the world in touch with God somehow. This he did by a descending scale of "powers." These are probably best interpreted as attributes of God, yet they are not entirely foreign to the late Jewish scheme of angelology. In no case are they to be thought of as lesser deities.

> At the peak is God; in the second position comes the Logos; in the third the creative power; in the fourth the directive (kingly) power; fifthly, under the creative, the power which conserves and oversees; in sixth place, under the directive, the power to punish; in seventh place, and lastly, the world composed of ideas. (*On Exodus*, 2,68)

Philo's Logos is like the Demiurge or Craftsman responsible for Plato's universe. It is Stoic-like in that it can be interpreted as the mind of the Lord through which he creates all things ("according to pattern," in the Stoic system.) Human spirits speak to the spirit of him in whose image and likeness they are made. He is knowable to men insofar as he is Logos. The perfect know God by mystical intuition; others less perfect have only the way of the Logos open to them. Philo is disconcerting in his variety of identification of the "powers" he proposes. Sometimes the creative power is the "God" of the Scriptures and the directive power "the Lord"; at times the powers will be three, five, or infinite in number, but all divine; at still other times they will be angels or ministering spirits. The Logos figure is the most ambiguous of all, seemingly being an intermediary between the Infinite and the finite, between Creator and creature. At no time is the Logos clearly a creature of God. Much less is he a second divine person. The term scarcely has personal force for Philo, even when he speaks of "first-begotten Son." He means to equate it with the archetypes immanent (*Lógos prophorikós*) in God's mind, which are expressed (*endiáthētos*) by his acts of creation and providence.

What emerges clearest of all is that like others of the Jewish world of his time this religious thinker has fixed on a scheme of mediators, and one in particular, to bring the Lord closer to his world—that world to which no prophet had been sent in centuries. Philo does not entertain even briefly the idea of the incarnation of a personal Logos. There is no observable relation between his teaching and the Johannine doctrine of the Word, except that both had access to a common fund of Old Testament and Hellenistic ideas. The Word for John is a person intimately conjoined to the Father, coming forth from him and going back to him. For Philo the word was a concept, an idea. This ambitious philosophical notion did not succeed in bridging the gulf between God and man for many persons other than his most philosophically-minded contemporaries. It would be quite mistaken in us to suppose that Philonian thought represented a large or influential segment of Jewish religious thought.

THE NEW TESTAMENT DATA

The Synoptic Gospels on Jesus' Divine Status

A cursory, or indeed a careful, examination of the three synoptic gospels (completed in their present form ca. 80 A.D.) discloses that they contain no explicit mention of the three divine persons except for the passage at the end of Matthew. (Mt 28,19) This so-called "missionary command" of the Lord, as it was transmitted in the Palestinian churches, gives some evidence of being a developed liturgical formula of baptism. An inspired writer in the Palestine community had produced canonical Matthew, which is widely presumed to have been the Greek redaction of an Aramaic original (though a few substantial scholars hold otherwise). It is, in any case, faithful to the spirit of that apostle's teaching. Up to that point in the synoptic gospels, one chiefly learns from Jesus' lips the master idea of the trinitarian revelation: that the Lord of Israel is his Father in a special and even unique way. (Cf. Lk 2,49, where "my Father" is set off from Mary's description of Joseph as "your father"; Mt 12,50, in which Jesus' relation to his "heavenly Father" completely transcends his relation to his earthly "brother, sister, mother"; Mt 20,23; 25,34; Lk 22,29; 24,49.)

Jesus underscores strongly a teaching of the Scriptures that has failed to come through to his contemporaries in its net effect, despite certain passages of great beauty. The Lord had said of Israel (Ephraim) that although "I stooped to feed my child, they did not know I was their healer." (Os 11,4) Malachia (2,10) likewise had spoken of "the one God who created us" as "Father." That men have in God a loving Father, not just a father-figure of authority, is a point Jesus is at considerable pains to make. (Mt 6,6–15.25–32) The idea of God's fatherhood is certainly central to the sayings-collection known as the Sermon on the Mount. It remains for the fourth gospel to give us Jesus quite clearly distinguishing between "my Father and your Father" (Jn 20,17) in a non-equivocal sense. As for the Spirit in the first three gospels, he is someone who of old inspired David and the prophets (Mk 12,36), and who impels the figures in the story of salvation including Jesus himself to their courses of action. (Lk 1,15.41.67; Mk 1,12; Lk 4,14)

Clearer by far, however, than the distinctness of the idea of Spirit from the idea of God in the synoptics is the claim Jesus made to be Son on terms of intimacy and equality unheard of in the Old Testament and even the intertestamental apocalyptic literature. The term "son of God" does appear, although rarely, in documents such as the *Psalms of Solomon* (13,8; 17,30; 18,4) and in an as yet unpublished Dead Sea scroll—in a far stronger attribution—to describe someone who enjoys the Lord's favor in a special way. The generous almsgiver is likewise called a "son of the Most High" in Sirach 4,10. On Jesus' lips, however, there is no doubt that it is more than an honorific title for the Messia. The evangelists designate him "son of God," reflecting the belief of the early Church. (Mk 1,1; 15,39; Jn 1,49) His own favorite title for himself is the enigmatic "son of man" (Mt 17,12; 20,18f; 24,30; 26,64; Jn 1,51), yet he comes to be honored after his death as the Son of God in a more than attributive and analogous sense. In the most primitive of the gospels, Mark, the unclean spirits accord him the title of "Son" or "Holy One of God" (Mk 1,24; 3,12; 5,7); Simon gives it to him in the theologically more developed Matthew. (16,16) All three synoptics (Mk 12,1–9; Mt 21,33–41; Lk 20,9–16) contain the parable of the wicked vinedresser, in which the owner's "only son" is unmistakably Jesus himself, while the owner can be no other than the Lord of Israel, and the other emissaries Israel's prophets.

Jesus does not hesitate to see in himself David's master whom Yahweh the Almighty will seat at his right hand. (Mk 12,35ff) Finally, he is found guilty of blasphemy when he permits the high priest to call him "the son of the Blessed One." (Mk 14,61; Mt 26,63) Had he made some distinction between this high title and that of Messia some mitigation of the charge is conceivable; in any case he made none. Even when he is claiming ignorance of the Last Day because it is not in the Father's plan to reveal it, his phrasing is significant: "neither the angels in heaven, nor the Son, but the Father only." (Mk 13,32) All other men by exclusion are in a separate category from himself. Jesus utters a blessing (*berakah*) upon the return of his disciples, "trembling for joy in the Holy Spirit" at what the Father has revealed to the simple concerning the mystery of the kingdom: "Yes, Father, for such was your good pleasure. All things have been delivered to me by my Father; and no one knows who the Son is except the Father, and who the Father is except the Son, and him to whom the Son chooses to reveal him." (Lk 10,21f) The person of Jesus is known to God only; but since any man can claim as much he adds the reciprocal feature which makes this particular Father-Son relation unique: the God of Israel is known to Jesus only, in such a way that he alone has the power to reveal him to others.

Jesus' Sonship of God in the Gospel According to John

The fourth evangelist's testimony on the relation of Jesus to God is frequent and explicit. He speaks of a Word "who was in the beginning with God . . . who was divine." (In 1,1f *theós,* the usual New Testament word for God the Father, is used with the definite article but elsewhere without it; grammarians are divided as to whether or not a difference of meaning is intended in the two usages.) The word is "with" him in the sense of being directed toward him (*pròs,* v.2), in his inmost being (*eis tòn kólpon,* "bosom," v.18). More than that, twice in this prologue he is called the "only Son" of the Father (*monogenēs.*) Jesus claims to pre-exist Abraham, using the verb redolent of the divine name in the Mosaic theophany of Ex 3,14, "I am." (Jn 8,58) He is a being "from above" (8,23) for the fourth evangelist, "the son of man who is in heaven." (3,13) He tells what he has seen with his Father. (8,38) The claim is comprehended sufficiently; he is stoned for "making himself God." (10,33) God has sent his Son into the world not to judge it but to save it. (3,17) Knowledge of the Son is as important to gain eternal life as knowledge of the Father. (17,3) The Son depends on the Father completely; he can do nothing apart from him. (4,34; 5,19; 6,58; 8,29; 12,49f; 17,1f) Judgment is already passed on the resistant because they have hated "me and my Father." (15,24) There is to be no sorrow among Jesus' disciples at his return to God "because the Father is greater than I." (14,28) In other words, when their close friend has returned to the Source of all, who sent him on his saving mission, they must rejoice at their new intimacy with the God of Israel whom they now know as Jesus' Father and as theirs. Jesus is in the Father and the Father is in him. (14,10) To see him is to see the Father (v.7); their words and works are always done in concert.

The discourse of Jesus at the supper table (Jn 14–17), from which the three quotations directly above are taken, is an extended claim to intimacy with God that no prophet or sage in Israel would dream of making. Jesus has given his friends a share in the glory his Father has *17* given him, "that they may all be one as we are one, I in them and you in me." (17,22f) He wills all to be one, "as you, Father, are in me and I am in you." (v.21) Jesus' use of the vine-and-branches figure, of himself as light of the world and as the life of men, when for the Israelite only Yahweh was to be thought of as the source of knowledge and the source of life, indicates that he thought of himself as intimately conjoined to the principle or "ground" in the divine. He is revealer and interpreter of one who is source and origin with respect to himself; yet at no time does he feel himself radically "subject," least of all in a creature-Creator relation, to him whom he calls Father.

The Holy Spirit in the New Testament

We have already pointed out that the Holy Spirit does not stand out sharply in the synoptic gospels from the Old Testament "spirit of the Lord." Things attributed to him could quite readily be taken as the works of God, for example the events attending the virginal conception of Jesus (Mt 1,18) and his presentation in the Temple (Lk 2,25), though the Holy Spirit's ubiquity here by name, including the use of the adjective fairly consistently, is worthy of attention. Jesus refers to him specifically as an ally in the persecution that is sure to come. (Mk 13,9ff) Blasphemy against him is particularly malicious (Mt 12,31f), raising the question of who he may be if he is not Yahweh himself nor the Son of Man. Mysterious though the Spirit is in his first New Testament appearances, he is always a distinct subject of attribution, and what is attributed to him is the very work of holiness which is the mission and message of Jesus from the Father.

In the fourth gospel the word "spirit" is of fairly frequent usage as contrasted with "flesh" (Jn 3,5; 4,24; 6,64), in contexts where the work of God or heaven is antithetical to the work of man or his proper sphere earth. The springs of living water that well up in anyone who believes in Jesus (7,38) are identified by the evangelist with the Spirit, "who had not yet come because Jesus had not yet been glorified." (v.39) The reference here is obviously to that full outpouring of the Spirit that would follow upon the Son's glorious return to the Father.

It is only at the last supper discourse that the person and work of the Spirit become fully explicit. The Father will send another Advocate

in response to Jesus' prayer, who will be with his friends always. (Jn

14,15ff) He is the Spirit of truth whom the world cannot receive because it has not known him. He will teach all that is needful, and recall to the disciples' minds the message of Jesus in its entirety. (14,25f) Jesus calls him "the Advocate . . . whom I will send you from the Father" (15,26), the same who before had been he "whom the Father will send in my name." (14,26)

Joint action in the work of mission is obvious, though Jesus' description of him as "the Spirit of truth who proceeds from the Father" (Jn 15,26) helps to create the problem of the *"filioque"* in the creed of Constantinople through what it leaves unsaid. (Cf. pp. 95ff below.) Although Jesus' return is made a condition of the Spirit's coming (16,7), and although "he will glorify me because he will receive from what is mine and proclaim it to you" (v.14), it is nowhere said in so many words that the Holy Spirit proceeds from the Son. The Father alone is the absolute point of origin. If the Spirit is sent by the Son it is "from the Father." His work is to console hearts at the loss of Jesus and consolidate all the gains Jesus has made in hearts. The work of the Two is clearly one, a work that originates with the Father. Nor are the Son and Spirit identical, even though Jesus says, "I am coming again." (14,3.18) The Spirit is one who will descend on those who possess the Son by faith and obey his commands. (14,16) The same condition attends the inhabitation of the Father: "If anyone love me, said Jesus, he will keep my word and my Father will love him, and we will come to him and make our abode with him." (14,23) The Three are therefore quite distinct yet closely associated in person and function. From the Father the others come forth, the Son as revealer and the Spirit as finisher of a task that is proper to all but primarily to the Father.

Specifically Trinitarian References in the Synoptics

Following this analysis of the persons taken singly in the four gospels, mention needs only be made of those passages other than the explicit liturgical formula of Matthew 28,19 where the Three appear to be spoken of in conjunction. One thinks immediately of Gabriel's announcement to Mary (Lk 1,35) where there is mention of the Holy Spirit and the power of the Most High, both Old Testament names for Yahweh, who (together?) shall effect it that the Holy One to be born of her will be *19* called "Son of God." There are the accounts of Jesus' baptism (Mk 1,9–11) and his transfiguration (Mk 9,2–9), both of which give the testimony of the Father and of the Spirit to the mission of Jesus. A profound literary kinship exists between the two accounts in all the synoptics. One sees in them the conviction of the primitive Church—whose catechesis the gospels were—that the mystery of Christ was inseparable from the mystery of the Father and of the Holy Spirit. Jesus is the "only Son" of his Father; the Father's good pleasure rests on him. (Mk 1,11) The Father gives his witness to the Son's person and message, and the sanctifying Spirit concurs in it fully.

The Acts of the Apostles

In the early chapters of Acts (written ca. 63) we have authentic accounts of the Church's primitive proclamation of faith. Her early preachers are not trinitarian in so many words, their stress throughout being on the glories of Jesus as "Lord and Christ" (Ac 2,36; 10,36; 20,21), but the divine Spirit's role is never forgotten. The first title of Jesus is clearly divine in context (kýrios); the other is a claim to the Messiaship of Israel. In Jesus of Nazareth alone is there salvation—this one whom the Father has raised up from the dead in the Holy Spirit. (Ac 2,24; 4,10)

The word "God" (theós) always describes the Father in Acts. Jesus is his Servant (paîs) whom he has glorified. (Ac 3,13.26; 4,30) The Holy Spirit has anointed Jesus with power and been with him in his cures and exorcisms. (10,38) The latter's humanity is stressed throughout, but as is the case with the words and deeds of Jesus reported in the gospels, his relation with God is described in Acts as mystifyingly intimate, and the Holy Spirit is never absent from it. Jesus' early disciples call him "Lord," they pray to him and consider him to be sovereign over human life. (5,14; 9,42) In their eyes, he has come into possession of all these rights in virtue of his resurrection. (5,31; cf. Gal 1,1.) This is the decisive sign whereby God gives proof that his crucified Servant now shares fully in his eternal glory.

The Holy Spirit's role is equally stressed throughout the Book of Acts. From the moment of his fiery descent to give wisdom and knowledge of Jesus (Ac 2,3ff), he is the guiding force of truth and holiness in the early community. (5,9; 8,29; 10,19.44–48; 11,12) He leads the

20

disciples to prospective believers and opens hearts. The first formal decree of the apostolic company at the so-called "council of Jerusalem" is issued in concert with the Holy Spirit. (15,28) There is no doubt that he is a personal divine force, the same one promised by Jesus and distinct from *theós*, the Father. Paul's ministry is unthinkable apart from the guidance of this Spirit. (13,2ff; 16,6f; 20,22) He it is to whom is attributed in its entirety the work of forming the band of believers in the image of Christ.

The Three Persons in Paul's Writings

When Paul in his letters comes to engage in a *teaching* about Christ, it is more developed theologically than the early *preaching* (or proclamation). He is closer to being professedly trinitarian, in other words. He never yields an inch in his loyalty to Hebrew traditions. (Phil 3,5) Monotheism is for him a necessary conclusion from the panorama of creation. (Rom 1,18ff) Yet the work of salvation is the work of Three: the Spirit of God leads those who are sons of God (not "sons of the Spirit") to the condition of coinheritance with Christ. (Rom 8,14ff) God and fatherhood are coterminous for Paul. (2 Cor 1,3f; Eph 3,14) God is both Father of all and Father of Jesus Christ in a unique way. Jesus is his Son, not by adoption as we are, but by nature. (Gal 4,4; Rom 8,3.32; Col 1,13) This sonship is a thing proper to Jesus, pre-existent as he is, before ever he was sent to earth by the Father (1 Tim 1,15; 2 Cor 8,9), but also a title he earned in a special way at his resurrection. (Rom 1,4) In no sense is it given him as a gift, as adoptive sonship is given to us. Before the incarnation Jesus is "equal to God." (Phil 2,6) There is a slight Stoic ring, as we shall see in Chapter Two, to Paul's exposition of the Father-Son relation, when he calls him

> the image of the invisible God, the firstborn of every creature; for in him everything has been created whether in the heavens or on the earth, things visible and invisible, whether thrones, dominations, principalities, powers . . . he is, before all things; they all subsist in him. (Col 1,15f)

Creation and conservation are works in which the Son has a part. He has "the form of God" (Phil 2,6), that is, the divine nature was his from the first; yet there is a sense in which God is other than he. Christings *21* in the flesh is "God, blessed forever" (Rom 9,5) in one reading of Paul's doxology, though others hold that this phrase from Paul's pen is unthinkable. Paul prays to Christ as to God (2 Cor 12,8f; 1 Tim 1,12; 2 Tim 4,18); he puts him on a level with God. (Gal 1,1) Snatches of rhythmic prayers to Jesus as Lord "glorified in high heaven" appear in the pastoral epistles. (Cf. 1 Tim 3,16.) The traditional phrasing of the early Church, however, always describes our approach to God as being in or through Jesus Christ. (Col 3,17; 2 Cor 1,20)

St. Paul's concern for the distinctness and divine character of the Spirit is no less than that of St. Luke, the author of Acts. The Spirit is sent by the Father and he is sent by the Son; he is the Spirit of the Father and the Spirit of the Son, or Lord. (Cf. Rom 8,9–14; 1 Cor 2,11; 2 Cor 3,17f.) The believer is a "temple of God" and a "temple of the Holy Spirit" indiscriminately. (1 Cor 3,16) At times it is not easy to distinguish clearly what use Paul is making of *"pneûma"* (spirit), all the letters in the Greek codices of the New Testament being majuscules. He will play on the word consciously, making it now mean the subsistent divine person, now the human individual who lets the Spirit work in him, again the principle within that person who has let himself be raised by God above the level of "flesh." That both the Son and the Spirit are distinct from the Father, yet fully God along with him, there can be no doubt. St. Paul is not a witness to the precise nature of the trinitarian mystery, but he is an indisputable witness to the trinitarian fact. It is providential that a Pharisee who outstripped many of his Jewish contemporaries in his devotion to the traditions of his ancestors (cf. Gal 1,14), should have given this testimony, rather than a Hellenized Jew of Philo's type.

Paul, the redoubtable monotheist, reflects the faith of the Christian community (in its own eyes not a sect or party but the true Israel), when he writes: "The grace of our Lord Jesus Christ, and the charity of God, and the fellowship of the Holy Spirit be with you all. Amen." (2 Cor 13,13[14]) Time and again in doxologies or discussions of gifts and functions within the Church, his wording will be professedly triune. Thus, "There are varieties of gifts but the same Spirit; and there are varieties of ministries but the same Lord; and there are varieties of roles but the same God, who works all things in all." (1 Cor 12,4ff) There is some evidence, it is true, for what has been called a "binitarian concern" (Eph 1,1f; Phil 1,1f), but Paul's devotion to the Holy Spirit in other places is such as to put beyond question his overall conviction that God is One in Three. (Cf. Gal 4,6; Eph 5,18ff.)

THE TRINITY REVEALED
WITH A VIEW TO MAN'S SALVATION

The uniqueness of the revelation of the three persons in God in the New Testament can be understood only in the context of the whole history of salvation. God's dialogue with man over the ages—chiefly through his action in history, which required a free and responsible answer on man's part—was the working out of a plan, a purpose (Eph 1,9; 3,9ff), a will or counsel (Ac 20,27; Eph 1,11; Heb 6,17) eternally foreordained (Ac 2,23), which came to its fullness only in Christ. With Christ's advent the "last days" (Heb 1,2) were ushered in, the "fulfillment of the ages" (1 Cor 10,11) was realized. In the opening words of Mark's gospel, with Jesus Christ's proclaiming of the good tidings "the time is accomplished." (Mk 1,15)

The climax of God's revelation is now definitive. Never again will his plan to save men be surpassed. This *final act* of salvation is accompanied by a new and *final revelation*. What had until then been a veiled secret is revealed: the inner life of Father, Son, and Spirit. The Johannine phrase "God is love" (1 Jn 4,16) means not merely that in his dealings with men is God loving but that his inner life is love. He is love in himself, a union and giving among three persons. The manifestation of love he makes in our regard is a communication of the love that he himself is. The "definitive reality," as K. Rahner calls the incarnation, means

> the indissoluble, irrevocable presence of God in the world as salvation, love and forgiveness, as communication to the world of the most intimate depths of the divine Reality itself and of its Trinitarian life: Christ. ("The Development of Dogma," in *Theological Investigations*, I, 49)

Revelation is said to be "closed" after the revelation made in Christ only because everything has been said, everything given "in the Son of Love, in whom God and the world have become one . . ." (*Ibid.*)

The New Testament writers fail to provide any set of abstract truths about the Trinity,[2] much less about the mystery of inner-trinitarian life,

---

[2] The word "trinity" to describe the three persons in God first appears as *triás* in the letter of Theophilus of Antioch *To Autolycus*, 2,15 (ca. 180 A.D.). Since he does not stop to explain it (the three days which preceded the creation of the sun

because they are constantly proclaiming the deed of God by which this fact and life are made known: "God so loved the world that he gave his only-begotten Son, that those who believe in him may not perish, but may have everlasting life." (Jn 3,16) The transmission of that life and the revelation of its essential trinitarian character are the one thing for the New Testament writers. Never do they conceive the mystery as revealed merely for the sake of knowledge, but to give man a share in the life of the Three.

The Three are revealed within the framework of God's eternal plan to save man, not through any precise terms such as person, nature, and substance. Consider Paul's opening chapter of Ephesians, one of his last letters to be written (62–63 B.C.):

> Praise be to the God and Father of our Lord Jesus Christ, who has bestowed on us in Christ every spiritual blessing in the heavenly realms. In Christ he chose us before the world was founded . . . to be full of love; and he destined us—such was his will and pleasure—to be accepted as his sons through Jesus Christ, that the glory of his gracious gift . . . might redound to his praise. . . . He has made known to us his hidden purpose . . . that the universe, all in heaven and on earth, might be brought into a unity in Christ. . . . When you heard the message of truth, the good news of your salvation, and had believed it . . . you became incorporate in Christ and received the seal of the promised Holy Spirit; and that Spirit is the pledge that we shall enter upon our heritage, when God has redeemed what is his own, to his praise and glory. (Eph 1,3–14)

In this passage the role of each of the Three in the work of our salvation is brought out clearly: the initiation by the Father, the mediatory role of Christ, and the sanctifying action of the Holy Spirit. The work to be accomplished by God is our adoptive sonship in Christ; the end, God's "praise and glory."

As has been said, the Father is *God* above all for Paul. It is doubtful that he ever refers to Christ as "God." (But cf. Rom 9,5; Tit 2,13.) The Father's role in the plan of salvation is one of initiation. He sent the Son

---

and moon "were types of the Triad, that is, of God and of his Word and of his Wisdom"), we must assume it was already a familiar term. Tertullian is the first to use the Latin word *trinitas*. (*Against Praxeas*, 3,11,12) Since the usage is not a part of primitive Christianity in either tongue, its introduction testifies somewhat to the conviction of the West about the unity of the divine substance. The East will stress more the distinctness of the persons, though it will not reject the word *triás*. In general, however, both words mean three of anything and we would err in attaching *too much* significance of oneness to this word.

24

into the world while we were still sinners (Rom 5,8f), raised Christ from the dead and exalted him above all creatures (Phil 2,5–11), gives us the grace of sonship through him and sees in him the end (*tò télos*) of the plan of salvation (1 Cor 15,24–28), which is "his hidden purpose." (Eph 1,9) God is "the Father" for St. Paul primarily because he is the "Father of our Lord Jesus Christ." (Rom 15,6; cf. Eph 1,3.) This fatherhood or family principle (*patriá,* Eph 3,14) is essential to God (the Father). It is not defined in relation to our adoptive sonship, but to Christ's natural sonship. The former is based entirely on the latter. We are sons because Christ is the Son, and heirs only because we are "in Christ." (Rom 6,11; 12,5) In the Old Testament Israel becomes God's son (Ex 4,22f; Os 11,1); Paul introduces the idea of our adoption (Rom 8,15.23; 9,4; Gal 4,5; Eph 1,5), not in the pagan sense of "God's offspring" but in a Roman legal sense. To this transaction, which empowers us to address God as "Abba," Father, the Holy Spirit is the witness-at-law.

God exercises his paternity, in Paul's thought, in three distinct spheres: creation, grace, and his own inner life. Paul gives his greatest attention to the sphere of grace. *We learn the interior trinitarian relations only incidentally to that.* This close relation between the work of our salvation and the activity of the Three who achieve it will later result in the heretical tendency known as "economic trinitarianism," the notion that God is not Three in essence but only in operation. (Cf. pp. 35,39 below.)

Paul's full faith in Christ is to be found in the two Christological hymns of Colossians 1,15–20 and Philippians 2,5–11. In the first he is the "image of the invisible God," the "firstborn of all creaturehood," the one "in," "for," and "through" whom all things have been created. He is the "beginning," the "head of the body"; in him the complete being of God (*plē'rōma,* v.19) came to dwell, so that through him alone (i.e., through the blood of his cross), peace and reconciliation between God and all things might be achieved. Christ therefore has first place in the orders of creation (vv.15f) and salvation. (vv. 18b–20) He is simultaneously God's image, someone essential to the act of creation, and head of the Church—all three.

The second hymn is even more explicit. "Divine nature was his from the first" has been proposed as a rendition of the familiar phrase which says Christ was "in the form of God." (Phil 2,6) Because he made himself nothing and assumed the nature of a slave, accepting in obedience even death, God raised him to the heights. His name is supremely praiseworthy. The cry goes round to the glory of the Father, "Jesus Christ is Lord." (v.11) We see three stages in the life of Jesus for Paul: the eternal pre-existence of the Son with the Father, his historical appearance on earth in the form of a man, and his glorious exaltation as the risen Christ. The cycle from heaven to earth and back to heaven again is one of majesty, humiliation, and glorification.

Throughout Paul's Christological teaching the personality of the Holy Spirit remains obscure. Paul shares the conviction of the early Church that the Spirit is outpoured in the Messianic day. "The charity of God has flooded our inmost heart through the Holy Spirit he has given us." (Rom 5,5) When God's kindness and generosity as Savior dawned on the world, "he saved us through the water of rebirth and the renewing power of the Holy Spirit." (Tit 3,5) The next verse says that he sent down the Spirit on us plentifully through Jesus Christ our Savior. Moreover, membership in the Church is "fellowship in the Holy Spirit." (2 Cor 13,13) He is the principle of life and power in Old Testament usage, but also particularly of holiness. He ensures that we are sons of God, as indicated above. (Gal 4,4–6; cf. Rom 8,14–16.) No one can say "Jesus is Lord" except under his influence. (1 Cor 12,3) Christian life is a matter of being guided or led by the Spirit. (Gal 5,16.18) "If the Spirit is the source of our life, let the Spirit also direct our course." (Gal 5,25) He explores everything, "even the depths of God's own nature. . . . Only the Spirit of God knows what God is." (1 Cor 2,10f)

The New Testament teaching on God's love is chiefly the unfolding of his desire to share with man the intimate relations of the trinitarian life. We are called to be sons to the Father and brothers to the Son in the loving union of the Holy Spirit.

> Every good comes to us from the Father, through Jesus Christ His incarnate Son and by means of the presence in us of the Holy Spirit; and similarly it is by means of the presence within us of the Spirit and through Christ that everything returns to the Father. . . . The Father reveals Himself essentially as the one from whom (*a quo*) and to whom (*ad quem*), the Son as the one through whom (*per quem*), and the Holy Spirit as the one in whom (*in quo*). (C. Vagaggini, *Theological Dimensions of the Liturgy*, p. 110)

In brief, we may say that the Scripture is less concerned with the
26 Trinity in itself than with its relation to the world, that is, our salvation. There God teaches man about himself gradually and through concrete

acts. Through his own actions, but chiefly through the Son he sends whose mission and work he seals (or confirms) in the Spirit, we know him. The point of departure is always the divine person, and the person in act. The apostolic company and the inspired New Testament writers came to know the divine Three one by one. Contemplating the work of salvation they come to see something of the inner relations of the divine life: the unity of nature, we would say, and the equality among the persons. These ideas they expressed somewhat vaguely yet always unmistakenly, since without interruption they were under the guidance of the Holy Spirit.

The knowledge of the Trinity which we have from the New Testament is above all personal. We are introduced to the Three and invited to share the happiness of the divine company. This is truly the great mystery of Christianity, the mystery of love. In the New Testament there is none of the remoteness in conceiving God which today tends to separate Christians from their triune Lord. The first Christians did not so much know God as one who, Father, Son, and Holy Spirit, had acted to save them, but as the God who had acted definitively to save them, through his Son, in the Holy Spirit.

"Then a cloud appeared, casting its shadow over them, and out of the cloud came a voice: This is my Son, my Beloved; listen to him." (Mk 9, 7) (Armenian illuminated manuscript 50.3; courtesy Freer Gallery of Art, Smithsonian Institution, Washington, D.C.)

CHAPTER TWO

THE EXTRA-BIBLICAL WITNESS OF THE FIRST THREE CENTURIES

We have indicated in the first chapter that the witness of the New Testament is clear on a variety of triadic formulas, none of which is explicitly "trinitarian." In other words, no theology of the trinity of persons in God had been developed by the time the canonical collection of Scriptures was closed. There are, it is true, triadic formulations proper to late Judaism and early Christianity which are rooted in the oneness of God without any overtones of distinctness of persons, for example one God—one name—one Israel; or one God—one Israel—one temple. (Cf. A. E. Suffrin, "God (Jewish)" in Hastings' *Encyclopedia of Religion and Ethics*, 6,295.) In the sub-apostolic period we encounter one God—one law—one hope. (*Pseudo-Clementine Homilies*, 3,17) St. Paul does a similar thing when he speaks of one Lord—one faith—one baptism (Eph 4,5), though on inspection it will be seen that there are seven members in this formula, three of them being Spirit, Lord, and Father; likewise faith—hope—charity. (1 Cor 13,13; Col 1,4ff; 1 Thes 5,8) There are as many dyadic formulas current in the late Jewish period as triadic (e.g. one God—one people of God, 4 Ezra 8,7). Four-, five- and seven-member formulas are also commonplace. Thus, for example, we find in the writings of the Jewish historian Josephus (d. ca. 100 A.D.) one God—one people of God—one city of God—one temple—one altar. (*Antiquities*, 4,200f)

EARLY EMERGENCE OF A TRIAD OF PERSONS

With this tradition behind him, it is not surprising that Paul speaks of one body—one spirit—one hope of [their] calling—one Lord—one faith —one baptism—one God and Father of all. (Eph 4,4ff) Clement (1 Cor 46,6) and Justin (*Apology*, 1,6) refer to quaternities made up of Father, Son, and Spirit, plus a "calling" (Clement) or "angels" (Justin.)

The presence of angels in a list along with the Father and the Son (no Spirit) is a New Testament commonplace (Mk 13,32; 1 Cor 8,5f; 1 Tim 5,21; Apoc 1,4f), just as a simple Father-Son dyad is of frequent occurrence. (Cf. Mt 23,8–10, where Jesus claims to be the sole "Rabbi" or "Messia" who balances off the one God; 1 Tim 2,5, "one mediator"; 1 Cor 8,6, "one Lord, Jesus Christ".) In all these cases, both Jewish and Christian, the emphasis is on the oneness of God as expressed in the oneness of any given number of "sacraments" or visible tokens of him. Indeed, the oneness of Jesus under whatever title he is given is put forth as a special proof of the oneness of God.

As has been said in the first chapter, however, the prevailing New Testament pattern by all odds is one of a triad that is unmistakably personal. The early Church's baptismal formula, "in the name of the Father, and of the Son, and of the Holy Spirit" (Mt 28,19) can only mean that Son and Spirit are two who stand in some relation of equality to the

Father, as evidenced by the reiterated conjunction "and." If they are but other names for him who is the One, or mere creaturely manifestations, then language is somehow being tortured. Despite the New Testament's numerous doxologies to Father, Son, and Spirit—all of them based on the assumption that the one God of Israel is being praised thereby—and the indisputable triadic character of the earliest baptismal creeds, there was evidently a need felt in the early centuries for a more explicitly trinitarian statement.

The need was experienced most keenly by Christians of the fourth century, a period which witnessed the first fierce theological disputes over this mystery. Spain supplied the lack by an ingenious interpolation into Scripture known as the *Johannine comma.* (Cf. J. Lebreton, *Histoire du dogme de la Trinité,* I, 645.) This addition to 1 John 5,7f—for there is no longer any dispute about the authenticity of the original, shorter reading—is as follows (in italics):

> There are three that bear witness *in heaven:*
> *The Father, the Word and the (Holy) Spirit,*
> *And these three are one.*
> *And there are three that bear witness on earth:*
> The Spirit, and the water, and the blood;
> And these three are one.

The insertion does not mean that the initial sacred writer's triad (Spirit, water, blood) was not an echo of his belief about the inner nature of God; it might very well have been. What it does mean is that the Johannine wording lent itself admirably to the expression of a longed-for creedal formula of divine threeness in unity, which it ingeniously received at the hands of some nameless Spanish Christian as a result of the faith of the Church.

It should surprise us greatly if the triadic formulas proper to a variety of paganisms did not have an impact on late Judaism and early Christianity; and in fact it was so. The predominant idea was that of a family triad, father, spirit (female principle), and offspring. (Cf., e.g. *Gospel to the Hebrews,* 2,3,6f.) Other documents have this syncretistic notion, a falsification of the Christian triad from which the notion of a fruitful pair or a family is entirely absent. (*Acts of Thomas,* 39; Epiphanius *Heresies,* 34,20,2) The "Egyptian Gospel" has a falsification of another sort in its mention of "the self-subsistent Father, the self-sub-sistent Son, the self-subsistent Holy Spirit" (Epiphanius, *op. cit.,* 15), a phrase which the Sabellians and other modalist heretics were happy to use along with other confusions from the Christian apocryphal writings.

THE PERIOD OF THE APOLOGISTS

With this reference to modalism we threaten to get ahead of ourselves. The next work of this chapter must be to examine the mystery of the three persons in God as it was taught in the Judaeo-Christian period. In this earliest epoch of the Church, both Word and Spirit were referred to as "angels." (Cf. J. Daniélou, *Théologie du Judéo-Christianisme*, I, "Trinité et Angélologie," pp. 167–98.) On careful inspection the word angel (*malak*) is seen to designate any spiritual substances which are distinct from other such substances—"persons," we now say. A certain subordinationism crept into the early usage, for example Word and Spirit adore and praise God (*The Ascension of Isaia*, 9,40), in passages which later give support to the theologies of Origen and the Arians. Overall, however, the faith of the Church was such as came to be ratified after the Council of Constantinople in 381 (D86[150]) in the formula of one God existing in three coequal persons.

It must be remembered, of course, that biblical categories of thought were the only ones current in the Church until the middle of the second century. True, men who were learned in pagan philosophy such as Aristides (fl. 150) and St. Justin (d. ca. 165) used the knowledge they had had from early youth to prove that there was no inherent absurdity in the Christian gospel. This they did by contrasting it with "fables" and comparing it favorably with widely accepted philosophical opinions. Theirs was primarily philosophical argumentation, however. No true Christian "theology" emerged until the late second and early third centuries, when men like Origen (d. 253–4) and Clement of Alexandria (d. before 215) attempted to discuss the Christian mysteries with the aid of philosophical systems. Up until then there had been only apologies, and what may be termed the biblical theologies of Tertullian (d. after 220) and St. Irenaeus (d. ca. 210) who contented themselves—when they were not arguing apologetically—with expounding the meaning of the Scriptures.

The pre-theological period of the apologists was quite clear on God's unity, his almighty power, and his fatherhood understood in the sense that he was the font and origin of all. (Cf. Hermas, *The Shepherd*, 1,1;

32

Vision, 1,3,4; Clement, *1 Cor,* 19,2; *Letter of [Pseudo-] Barnabas,* 21,5; *Didachē,* 10,3.) There was nothing distinctively Christian about the God of the apologists; he was, of course, the one God, Father and Creator of Old Testament faith, but was conceived more philosophically than biblically, even to the use of Aristotle's argument from motion for God's existence. (Aristides, *Apology,* 1,4) This God sets all in order—a Stoic echo—yet is not to be confused with the world. It is he who contains the heavens, not they who contain him. God is *agénnētos* for Justin, *a term meaning unoriginated, in contrast to creatures who have a beginning.* (*1 Apology,* 14,1) *The importance of this Greek term cannot be overstressed.* It will recur constantly in the discussion of the mystery of the Trinity.

God is also eternal, changeless, impassible, and the cause of all existence, in the writing of Justin. All are terms from Greek philosophy; but the Hebraic titles "Creator" and "Father of all" go side by side with them in the writings of Justin, Theophilus of Antioch (*To Autolycus*), and other Christian writers of the period.

An absolute clarity emerges in these writings regarding the creation of the world by God out of nothing. Nothing created can be God, the authors maintain, and he cannot have in himself any element of having been produced from nothing. All things that are, God made through his Word out of nothing. It is proper to matter to be originate (*gennētós*); this notion is unthinkable with respect to God. The Platonic idea that matter existed from eternity received censure from the Christian apologists because non-origination is a property of God alone. His position as sole first principle (*monarchía*) would be threatened, they said, by eternal matter. The idea of "eternal creation" did not occur to them as an alternative, acceptable or otherwise. "From nothing God created whatever he willed," wrote Theophilus of Antioch, "as he willed it." (*To Autolycus,* 2,4)

We have said that the apologists, although in a strict sense pre-theological, were firm on the fatherhood of God. Often their rigorous monotheistic thought confined itself to a consideration of his fatherly role as Creator, but they were not without an explanation of the relation of Christ to the Father. As Word he had pre-existed time in the bosom of the Father, they knew from the fourth gospel. St. Ignatius of Antioch, similarly, had referred to Christ as the Father's Word spoken in silence. (*To the Magnesians,* 8,2) It was by way of an easy transition that the

33

second-century apologists came to speak of the coming forth of Son from Father in terms of Stoic vocabulary: the Word that had been immanent was uttered or expressed.

Justin's struggle with this concept resulted in his describing the Logos as the Father's intelligent or rational thought which was enfleshed in its entirety in Jesus Christ. (*1 Apol.,* 5,4) In his *Dialogue with Trypho* (128,4), he supplied the necessary corrective to this by saying that the Two are not distinct in name only, as the light is from the sun, but numerically (*arithmōi*) as well. The Logos is with the Father before all creatures, put forth as an offspring, and is divine. "He is adorable, he is God." (*Dial.,* 63,5) "We adore and love, next to God, the Logos derived from the increate and unutterable God . . ." (*2 Apol.,* 13,4) At various points in the three words cited above, Justin calls the Logos God's "child," his "offspring," and his "sole-begotten." The Father generates him by an act of will (*Dial.,* 61,1) in order to create and reveal through him, though Father and Son are not separated thereby. At this point the human word or idea serves Justin as an analogy: in a man who gives expression to the thought within him there is neither cutting off nor diminution.

Athenagoras was undoubtedly the first to press the idea of the Logos as the Father's rationality. (*Apology,* 10) According to Tatian and Theophilus of Antioch, this eternally reasonable (*logikós*) principle in God was given expression by an act of will. Like Justin they thought of the Word as the Father's instrument in creating and governing the universe, and in making man in God's image. Tatian entertained the confusion that at the creation the immanent Logos sprang forth from the Father as his absolutely first work. The emission of the eternally immanent Word before the creation was accomplished (all perfectly good Stoic terminology) caused the Church not a little grief in the period of the Arian threat. Meanwhile, the apologists were trying to see in Paul's "firstborn of all creation" (Col 1,15) that eternal Counsellor of the Lord who is his own intelligence and thought. "He did not [in engendering and bringing him forth] thereby empty himself of his Word, but having begotten him consorts with him always." (Theophilus, *To Autol.,* 2,22) The Word never actually came into being. Because the Father is eternally rational he has his Word in himself always.

It is important for us to see that, although the apologists were con-34 vinced that the rational Father always had his Logos with him for communion and counsel, they stressed his taking counsel with him only in times of need. The works of creation, revelation, and redemption comprised such need. We might be tempted, therefore, to accuse these early Christians of holding the merely "economic emission" or "production" of the Son, whereas in fact their belief in his eternal generation is firm. *It is simply that they saw the Father-Son relation more as it touches us—the only way we know of its existence—than as it is in the godhead itself.*

A second important matter is that divine fatherhood, in the sense of authorship of all that exists, was attributed by these second-century thinkers to the Father accompanied by his Word and his Spirit, rather than to the Father alone. Despite groping attempts like Justin's "second God" worshipped "in a secondary rank" (*1 Apol.*, 13,3) they never wearied repeating the oneness in essence of the Word with the Father, "inseparable in His fundamental being from Him as much after His generation as prior to it." (J.N.D. Kelly, *Early Christian Doctrines*, p. 101)

The apologists were less expressive on the person of the Spirit than on the Father and Son. He was "the prophetic Spirit" for them; someone who comes to dwell in the souls of those who live justly. Athenagoras called him an outpouring (*apórroian*) of God, and was not alone in likening the Spirit to a ray of the sun in his going forth from the Father and returning to him. (*Apology*, 7,2; 9,1) He was the inspirer of the prophets and the illuminator of hearts, though the Logos had the same function for several apologetic writers. At times spoken of in less than personal terms, the Spirit was a full sharer in the divine nature despite Justin's relegating him to the third "rank" of deity. This rank or order (*táxis*) does not connote subordination so much as the progressive manifestation of the persons in the plan of redemption. A delicate balance was maintained by these teachers who preceded theological activity proper, in their recognition of plurality in the divine, while at the same time teaching a manifestation in time of God's Word and his Wisdom (Theophilus' usage) which does not interrupt his essential unity.

THE EMERGENCE OF THEOLOGICAL THOUGHT
The Eastern Tradition

Whereas a philosophical confusion between God and his world was the major error which the apologists struggled against, Irenaeus, bishop of Lyons in Gaul, had to fight the opposite teaching of the Gnostics that a hierarchy of lesser divine beings (collectively the *plē'rōma* or fullness) bridged the abyss between the unthinkable Highest Power and the universe. These beings (or aeons) had as their chief member the creator god responsible for the visible world. Irenaeus opposed this conception strongly (*Against Heresies*, 2,1,1), saying that he alone who was God and Father and Lord had likewise been the Creator. God creates through his Word and his Wisdom, or Spirit. Not to speak of multiplying deities, the existence of the demiurge (creator, craftsman) of Gnosticism runs into the immediate difficulty that any such being has another superior or equal to himself, and therefore cannot be God.

The distinctive thing about the God of the Christians was that he had revealed himself in the person of Jesus the Messia, and subsequently poured out his Spirit on all who believed in that revelation. He was not multiple in any sense; lesser beings like to him did not emanate from his substance as part of him (the Gnostic position); neither was he so totally opposed to the world of matter that it was inconceivable he should have created it (the dualism taught by Marcion, d. ca. 165). Yet the person of Jesus was spoken of as early as New Testament times (we saw this in Chapter One) as pre-existing the world and having a part in its creation. The Spirit was similarly described as "justifying," "consoling," and "reconciling" man, all this without his threatening the oneness of the God who alone could perform these works, any more than the Word through whom all was made comprised a threat to the divine unity.

THE TRINITY IN EARLY LITURGIES AND DOXOLOGIES   Before there were any creeds in the Church such as that of Constantinople, there were semi-fixed formulas deriving from the apostolic proclamation of the redemptive fact: God had sent his Son who had been put to death, had risen, ascended to the Father, and would return in glory; the Spirit had inspired the prophets and other holy men of old to write in anticipation of these events. A triadic pattern gradually emerged in those loose declarations of the "rule of faith" that paralleled the earliest baptismal formulas (Mt 28,19; *Didachē* 7,1–3) and the creeds.

One such declaration, that of Irenaeus, follows:

> God the Father, not made, not material, invisible; one God, the creator of all things: this is the first point of our faith. The second point is this: the Word of God, Son of God, Christ Jesus our Lord, who was manifested to the prophets according to . . . the Father's dispensa-

tion; through whom all things were made; who also, at the end of the age, to complete and gather up all things, was made man among men, visible and tangible, in order to abolish death and show forth life and produce perfect reconciliation between God and man. And the third point is: the Holy Spirit, through Whom the prophets prophesied . . . who at the end of the age was poured out in a new way upon mankind in all the earth, renewing man to god. (*Demonstration of the Apostolic Preaching*, 6)

Earlier, St. Justin had described a baptism of regeneration in water, "in the name of God, the Father and master of all things . . . of Jesus Christ who was crucified under Pontius Pilate . . . and of the Holy Spirit, who foretold by the prophets the whole story of Jesus." (*1 Apology*, 1,10–13) The same writer reports a doxology which lay at the heart of the eucharistic canon: "Glory to the Father of all things, in the name of the Son, and of the Holy Spirit." (*Ibid.*, 65) *The Acts of Martyrdom of Polycarp* (14,3) gives a similar prayer: "I glorify You through the everlasting and heavenly high priest Jesus Christ, Your beloved Son, through whom be glory to You together with him and the Holy Spirit."

Unequivocal formulations of this sort marked the teaching of St. Irenaeus, the central figure of Christian orthodoxy in the lifetime before Origen. He avoided philosophical terms whenever possible, although he was considerably indebted to the apologists. Like them he viewed the Father as incomparably One, with whom eternally was his Word and his Wisdom. The latter were made manifest as Son and Spirit on the occasions of creation and redemption. "By the very essence and nature of his being there is but one God," he taught in his *Epideíxis* or *Demonstration* (47), while at the same time "according to the economy of our redemption there are both Father and Son." Irenaeus was clearer than his predecessors on the relation of the redemptive fact to the divine Three. He was very much in the spirit of the fourth gospel when he said "What is invisible in the Son is the Father, and what is visible in the Father is the Son." (*Against Heresies*, 4,6,3) Irenaeus did not have the theological notion of the eternal generation of the Son, but he did view the Word who was eternally with the Father as identical with him. In this he departed from an old analogy which saw the Word as distinct from God in the manner of a human idea distinct from the thinker. (*Ibid.*, 2,28,4ff)

Irenaeus's treatment of the Holy Spirit was quite satisfactory. He chose, with Theophilus and against Justin, to identify the Spirit with God's Wisdom rather than with his Word. This put at his disposal all 37 the texts of the Old Testament in which wisdom was personified, to teach the eternity of the third person and his close association with the Father in establishing all things. Aside from being the one through whom the prophets prophesied and the fathers learned the things of God, the Spirit was he without whom "it is impossible to behold the Word of God . . . since the knowledge of the Father is the Son, and the knowledge of the Son of God can only be obtained through the Spirit." (*Demonstration,* 7) Our holiness is likewise the doing of "the Spirit of the Father which purifies a man, and raises him to the life of God."

The Son's manifestation is the making known of the Father, Irenaeus taught. Again, he states very clearly: "The Father is God, and the Son is God, for whatever is begotten of God is God." (*Dem.,* 47) He never called the Spirit God directly, but supposed that since the Spirit was God's Spirit and had his being from the Father he had to have full divine status.

Throughout the late second and early third century writings of this saintly bishop of Lyons we find no mention of three coequal persons. This clarification would not come for another century. God (Father) was the one great personage who dwelt not alone but with his Mind, or Thought, and his Wisdom. He was thus mysteriously Three in One. Whereas his unity was preserved in this conception, the distinctness of the other persons was inadvertently suppressed or made subordinate to their role in the economy of salvation. Irenaeus, aware of this, clung as did his predecessors to the figure of a man and his spiritual or intellectual processes. They meant to preserve thereby the idea of real distinctions in the godhead that had been there from eternity—any manifestation through activity over the ages quite apart.

GOD'S UNITY AND TRINITY IN TENSION   St. Irenaeus provided the capstone of the religious thought-edifice of the first two centuries of the Church's life. His convictions about the inner life of God, summarized above, were to prove insufficient in the face of two opposing tendencies that came out clearly in the early third century. Among orthodox teachers, Origen provided certain clarifications in the East as did Tertullian in the West, but so unequivocal was each in representing the thought of his sector of Christendom that a further resolution was called for. The heretical teachings of Lucian of Samosata and Arius of Alexandria brought matters to a head, and led to the solution at Nicaea of 325.

As to the two tendencies spoken of, both of them found in the writings of Irenaeus, there was the irreformable Christian commitment to the unity of God and his distinction from creatures, and the equally clear conviction that in him existed a Triad. The latter term is chosen rather than "Trinity" in order to describe the Father, his Word, and his Wisdom without any connotation of the exact relations in which the Three eternally stand to each other. This work of theology had not yet been done, nor had any of the precisions of vocabulary as yet been made that would serve as vehicles for a speculative thought that had not up to this time been engaged in. The revelation of the Son and Spirit as other than the Father in the redemptive economy proved both a help and a hindrance in conceiving the trinitarian reality. It assured the divine Three a dynamic character in the thought and prayer life of Christians, but it cripplingly deferred exploration of the eternal relations of the Three.

This "economic trinitarianism," as we may conveniently call it, caused certain Christians to take fright at the stress on triplicity in the godhead. They were so dedicated to preserving the notion of the "monarchy," or divine unity-in-origination, that they looked on any notion of pluralism in the deity as a threat to pure monotheism. This was unfortunate because the emerging notion of three "persons" could always be tarred with the brush of tritheism (belief in three Gods). The unity of the godhead, contrariwise, could be described as modalism by those who opposed the monarchians. The term modalism, of course, refers to the notion that the Son and the Spirit were mere modes of being of the divine monarchy, made manifest specifically on the occasions of creation and salvation.

The Western Tradition

The colorful anti-pope Hippolytus (d. 235), famous for a traditionalist spirit which bordered on archaism, stuck a good balance in his efforts against the monarchian Noetus of Smyrna. We know of the latter's teaching chiefly from Hippolytus' treatise *Against Noetus* and the writings of Epiphanius a century later. Noetus was so firmly committed to the unity of God and the divinity of Christ that he seems to have seen in Christ's passion no more than the Father's suffering. For his *patripassianism* the presbyters of Smyrna arraigned him, and not all his innocent cries that he had simply taught that the one God, Christ, had suffered and died for us could save him from condemnation. We have

39

it from Hippolytus that Noetus and his disciple Epigonus, who subsequently came to Rome during the pontificate of Zephyrinus (198–217), taught an undifferentiated godhead that could be designated either Father or Son indiscriminately. (*Against the Heresy of Noetus,* 9–10) The names stood for no real distinctions.

Tertullian's adversary Praxeas, whoever he was, seems to have held the same position. The Father and Son were identical, "the Word" being a mere utterance of the lips. In the godhead there was realized a Heraclitean resolution of all opposites, so that invisibility and visibility, impassibility and passibility provided no problem for the Father. He became, so to say, his own Son in taking flesh of the Virgin. Hippolytus had affirmed of God that, "Though alone, he was multiple, for he was not without his Word and his Wisdom, his Power and his Counsel." (*Against Noetus,* 10) Tertullian goes further in pointing out that "before all things God was alone . . . in the sense that there was nothing external to himself. Even then he was not really alone, for he had with him that Reason which he possessed within himself, that is to say, his own Reason." (*Against Praxeas,* 5)

THE PERSONS KNOWN THROUGH GOD'S PLAN TO SAVE   An important contribution of these two thinkers, the one a Greek-speaking Roman and the other an African who wrote in Latin, is their use of *prósōpon* or *persona* to describe others than the Father in the deity. For Hippolytus, alongside the Father there is "another," a second "person," while the Spirit is yet a third in the Triad. (*Against Noetus,* 7; 11; 14) There is, however, only one God or All and one Power, the Word; it is the Father who commands in the "economy," the Son who obeys, and the Spirit who makes us understand.

It is evident from this how related to the saving event the trinitarian distinctions are for Hippolytus. He freely called the Word a Son only at the incarnation. Tertullian was likewise loath to call him Son until the creation, since his "perfect generation" dated only from his going forth from the Father to serve as the image or archetype of creatures, who would also be created through him. This going forth, incidentally, is conceived as willed by the Father, a primitive equation of the eternal Word with the divine act of will as against the vagaries of Gnostic emanationism.

40   The Word or Son is a *persona,* Tertullian said, "a second in addition to the Father." (*Against Praxeas,* 5) The Spirit in turn is a *vicaria vis*

or deputized agent of the Son (*On Prescription,* 13), who comes forth "from the Father through the Son." (*Against Praxeas,* 4) He is,

> third from the Father and the Son, just as the fruit derived from the shoot is third from the root, and as the channel drawn off from the river is third from the spring, and as the light-point in the beam is third from the sun. (*Ibid.,* 8)

The two third-century teachers were at pains to be explicit on the divine unity, though they simply could not satisfy the modalists on this point. They repudiated any idea of separation in God. Tertullian favored the term *distinctio* or *distributio.* Father, Son, and Spirit were one in "substance," he maintained. There was extension but no division. "I and the Father are *unum,*" he pointed out, quoting the Latin version of the fourth gospel, one reality; not *unus,* one person. From Tertullian we derive the phrase that the Son is "of one substance with the Father" (*Against Praxeas,* 2); the Son and the Spirit are "sharers" (*consortes*) in it (*ibid.,* 3); "the Father is the whole substance, while the Son is a derivation from and portion of the whole" (*ibid.,* 9). The Three are indivisibly one in status, substance, and power, is his final view. Only in rank (*gradus = táxis*), manifestation, or appearance can any threeness be attributed to them. This last idea is Tertullian's real contribution: oneness of substance coupled with plurality of expression or form. Both he in using *persona* and Hippolytus in using *prósōpon* had in mind the manifestions of Son and Spirit in the economy rather than individuals immanent in the eternal godhead. Neither ancient word connoted "person" in its modern sense. The etymological transition had been from face or expression, to a player's mask (*per + sonare*=to speak through), to an individual who held title to property at law. Tertullian means by the word "the concrete presentation of the individual as such." (Kelly, p. 115) It is providential that besides conveying the idea of distinct expression of a single nature or essence—its primitive task—"person" should be so well fitted to describe an individual possessor of the one indivisible godhead.

PROTECTORS OF GOD'S MONARCHY: THE MODALISTS   The monarchian position in some of its modalistic expressions has already been outlined. Basically it tried to protect the unity of the godhead by reducing Christ to the status of a mere man, and the Holy Spirit to a divine force.   *Adoptionism,* sometimes called dynamic monarchianism, was a Christological heresy which taught that the Spirit of God descended on Mary's son at his birth, or more usually, his baptism, enabling him to do the work for which he was sent. Its first protagonist is said to have been Theodotus of Byzantium, a learned merchant who brought it to Rome around 190. He was Catholic in much of his belief except for the key matter of the descent of the Spirit, or Christ, on the virtuous man Jesus at his baptism. Theodotus did not hold for Christ's deification at any time as some adoptionists did, usually on the occasion of his heavenly glorification. Pope Victor (186–98) excommunicated him, but his teaching was taken up by another layman of the same name. This rationalistic version of Christianity was put forward by men interested in science, mathematics, and medicine. They probably balked at the incarnation of the deity, finding it convenient to claim against Catholic faith that it held for two Gods, the Father and the Son.

The best known of the adoptionists is Paul of Samosata, a man whose precise teaching is not easy to isolate. We know that he was condemned at a synod of Antioch in 268 and that he was basically a unitarian who did not hesitate to employ traditional Christian formulas. His chief concern was Christological, not trinitarian. "Jesus Christ was one," he taught, "and the Word was another." The Word for him was a verbal utterance giving the divine command, not a divine *ousía* or subsistent individual. His judges evidently pointed out (we have only the later reports of Athanasius, Hilary, and Basil on the process), that the Word was one of three divine *ousíai,* to which he piously retorted that the Word was *homooúsios* with the Father, i.e. of the same *ousía,* not truly distinct from the one divine *ousía.* Paul's unitarian understanding of that term would doubtless include both the divine essence and individuality, there being no room in his system for a plurality of individuals. True to his own principles (we have this from a sixth-century reporter *On Sects*), he held the Spirit to be merely the grace that indwelt the apostles. He never held, it seems, as did certain other modalists, that in the working out of the economy Christ came forth from the Father as a subsistent person. Quite simply, Paul was an adoptionist through and through.

We have examined the somewhat unsophisticated monarchian modalism of the early third century (Noetus, Praxeas). Its wellspring was the twofold conviction of its proponents concerning the oneness of God and the full divine status of Christ. They could not resolve these propositions in any Catholic sense, but were only too ready to cry "two Gods" or "three" against any explicitation of the Logos doctrine that

42

ended in the distinctness of the Word and the Spirit from the Father. The Power coming forth from the Father (and remember, godhead equalled fatherhood in the first two centuries) had to be a projection of the Father, distinct from him only verbally. Any distinction "in number" aroused the protests of the monarchians even back in Justin's time. (*Dialogue*, 128, 3f)

SABELLIUS, PRINCE OF THE MODALISTS   The Catholic defense of the mystery of the Three by Hippolytus and Tertullian led to a framing of the modalist position on a more philosophical basis. This time the innovator was a certain Sabellius who came to Rome while Zephyrinus (d. 217) was still pope. He aroused the theological ire of Hippolytus but briefly won the favor of the latter's rival claimant to the papal throne, Callistus (217–22), who eventually excommunicated him. We must take our Sabellian teaching from the report of the much later orthodox writer Epiphanius (*Heresies*, 62,1,4), who tells us that for him the godhead was a single principle. Arius the heretic, in his *Letter to Alexander*, says he used the hybrid term *huiopatōr* to describe it: "Sonfather." There are three operations or successive projections in God (thus Sabellius): from one essence two modes of expression flow. Just as the sun yields light and warmth by radiation, so the Father projects himself first as Son and then as Spirit. As creator and lawgiver the one godhead is Father; as redeemer (Son) it went forth like a ray of the sun, to be withdrawn when the work was finished; as inspirer and bestower of grace the same godhead is Spirit. (Epiphanius, *Heresies*) Sabellius seems to be employing the orthodox features of a description of the Three at work in the economy while at the same time avoiding the patripassian charge. A century later the name of Marcellus, deposed bishop of Ancyra (d. 374), was linked with that of Sabellius; his teaching, however, was not a true nominalism or modalism but a theory of "expansion" of the pre-existent Logos from the single divine principle. Marcellus was, so to say, a last-ditch monarchian who could hold to his own terminology after Nicaea and still remain within the Catholic fold: an extreme "rightist" with respect to the divine unity against the background of the clear trinitarian language of the creed of 325.

THE STRUGGLE IN THE ROMAN CHURCH   Up until this point we have dealt exclusively with Fathers of the Church, ecclesiastical writers, and heretics who wrote in Greek, with the exception of Tertullian. This

43

is true even of Irenaeus in Gaul and Hippolytus in Rome. We have not yet reached that Greek-speaking Alexandrian, Origen, who is sometimes called the father of the science of theology. His trinitarian writings put the East unequivocally on the side of an emphasis on the distinction of the persons—the direction in which the East had long tended. Tertullian's struggle against modalism helped to give him balance on the question of the divine Three who were in no way to be confused. His philosophical tendency, however, like that of the rest of the Latin-speaking West, was toward the unity of the divine substance. We need to be grateful to this stormy petrel for his contribution, however "unofficial," to Western thought with its perpetual bent toward a theology of *monarchia* in the godhead. We have mentioned Popes Zephyrinus and Callistus who reigned in the quarter-century 198–222, both of them suspicious of Hippolytus and Tertullian. Their fear was that Christ's distinctness from God (Father) in the anti-modalist writings of the two tended to make a second God of him.

It seems to be the old story of the untutored men of faith, in this case shepherds of souls, who thought that it would suffice in all weathers to reiterate formulas from the faith of their youth. That the Sabellian threat required a more sophisticated response than "Christ is the one God who suffered for us" they did not fathom. All the talk of *prósōpa* and *personae* struck them as unscriptural and unnecessary. We know the faith of these two popes, it is true, only from Hippolytus' account of it in his *Refutation of All Heresies,* and he considered them modalist heretics. A more benign interpretation is doubtless truer to the facts: that they were sure that God was one and that Christ was fully divine, all this in the older monarchian tradition without any reference to the real distinction of Father and Son introduced in the second century. After all, Pope Callistus *did* excommunicate Sabellius. The latter's teaching must therefore clearly have departed from received Catholic forms of expression. The account we have of Callistus' teaching indicates that he was strongly committed to one divine spirit or reality. Although the Word existed before time, becoming the Son when he entered history, he was not "another alongside the Father." The Father was identical with the Word, indeed he became incarnate, but after that he only "co-suffered" with the Son. This wording seems to indicate a compromise spirit in Callistus which surely wishes to express *some* distinction between Father and Son, but not such as to rend the divine being into two.

44

ETERNAL SONSHIP FIRST TAUGHT APART FROM MAN'S SALVATION

The suggestive arguments of Tertullian ultimately prevailed, however. The papacy is by nature conservative of the traditions of the era immediately preceding. Who can say what mischief a Tertullian in Peter's chair (or an Hippolytus, though he thought he *was* there) might have done? Still, a theology of undifferentiated monarchianism was a threat to Catholic faith, and it is rewarding to observe that in the mid-third century a Roman theologian named Novatian achieved a breakthrough. In his treatise *On the Trinity* he went farther than Tertullian by teaching the generation from the Father of a Son, his Word, when the Father willed it. This Word has his own subsistence (*substantia*), being a second person. This is the first time that the pre-temporal Sonship of the Word is set free from the idea of creation. The Son receives his being from the Father in a "community of substance." As a "second person after the Father" he forever harks back to the Father. He is saved from being a second divine principle by being other than the Father only as Son. The *monarchía* is preserved, and in God there are Two. There are in fact Three for Novatian, but since his concern is with another problem he satisfies himself with the ancient modes of speech about the Spirit. The latter inspires the prophets, guides the apostles and the Church, and so on.

We call this a breakthrough because Novatian succeeded in making it clear, as no one before him had, that the Son's distinction from the Father was not something dependent on the mystery of man's salvation. He located the divine generation before time and apart from it. Even though the closest he came to the idea of eternal generation was to say that the Father always had his Son, and though he tended to subordinationism of the Son in his phrasing, he nonetheless set the inner life of God free from any consideration of time. His great concern continued to be protecting the godhead as the unique source of all reality. In this sense godhead is Father, and in this sense the Word derives from it.

It is interesting that we should hail this achievement of the year 250. The great need of the present period, paradoxically, is to recall the relation of the dynamic life within the Trinity to the economy of salvation. In the early centuries the disengagement of God from his world, and the Word and the Spirit from the Gnostic sub-pantheon, was the problem. The absolute unity of the divine substance seemed an adequate response to it, coupled with the fact of Christ's non-separation from this

one divine principle. With the supremacy of Western thought that resulted from the anti-Arian reaction, however (not so much in the fourth
century settlement itself), there came a serious need, which is still with
us in the West, to recall that the stress of the New Testament and all
primitive liturgies, Eastern and Western, is on the divine Three who act
to save us. Safe now in our heritage of certainty about the eternity of the
generation, procession, and mutual sharing in the godhead, we must turn
back to the earlier stress on the economy, or *how it all affects us*. Fortu-
nately, in the Church no treasure is lost—only mislaid for a few centuries,
or an occasional millennium.

The Alexandrian School

CLEMENT   It is impossible to know without an inquiry into the
theology of Origen (185–ca. 254) why the Council of Nicaea was so
desperately needed. The Western spirit had made its somewhat leisurely
way toward the synthesis of Novatian, reported above. Without the strong
Roman stress upon unity of the divine being, and without Tertullian's
anti-modalist checkmate, it could not have reached its early fourth-century
stage. The same is true of Origen's contribution to Eastern thought and
that of his Alexandrian predecessor by a generation, Clement. This pair
of thinkers in the Platonic tradition precipitated a formulation of the
Father-Son relation that was almost antipodal to that of Latin Christianity. Their intellectual histories were entwined with the revival of Middle Platonism in that exciting university city. The chief exponent of
this modified materialistic thought system, highly religious in orienta-
tion, was Origen's contemporary younger by twenty years, Plotinus.

Clement's career as a moralist, particularly, in the adult catechetical
school of the Egyptian metropolis, bore fruit in a variety of treatises. He
stressed allegory ("the pathology of typology") as the principle of biblical
interpretation; he rambled badly; at times he was barely orthodox. Clement's attention to the Triad was not extensive. It was a "wondrous mystery" to him how one who was Father of the universe—transcendent, inexpressible, incomprehensible—could be known only through his Word
or Son who was his image. This mind or rationality of God resembled
the *Nous* of Middle Platonic thought: God, the second *hypóstasis* to
come after the supreme One that was source of all. All that the Father
thinks, all that he does to animate his creatures, is summed up in the
Word. This Word is in the Father and is essentially one with him. "The

Father is not without his Son; for along with being Father, he is Father of the Son." (*Miscellanies,* 4,162,5) As to the Holy Spirit, he comes third in order and is the light and the power issuing from the Word. He illumines and attracts, this personal force who is not separated by division from either Father or Son.

Clement's teaching is Christian orthodoxy in Platonic speech, basically without new elements except for its stress on Christ as God's image (*eikōn*). Origen takes up the latter idea in the treatise that is the first systematic treatment of dogma, *On First Things* (1,2,6), which together with his work *Against Celsus* contains a complete synthesis of Christian faith and Middle Platonic thought. The originality of the attempt can fairly be compared to Aquinas's use of the philosophical categories of Aristotle to probe the Christian revelation. At times Origen seems too anxious to provide parallels at all points between faith and this philosophy. There is first of all, he says, a common divine substance shared by a second and third *hypóstasis* (an individual existent, for Origen). The Three are both eternal and far separated from any other beings brought into existence by the Father through the Word. They are not the only beings created eternally, however. A host of souls or spirits has been so created (the noblest is the human soul of Christ intimately conjoined to the Word); the mediator between the Father and all these eternal spirits is the Son or Word. He is God's express image containing in himself every aspect of human existence (wisdom, truth, life) and salvation (resurrection, healing.)

The distinctive feature of Origen's trinitarian teaching is the freedom with which he speaks of three separate *hypostáseis* or sometimes "things"; even "Gods, in one sense." The Father alone is "the fountainhead of dignity," God in the strict sense (*autótheos*), the sole ingenerate (*agénnētos*). The Son is begotten eternally—there never was a "when he was not." The Holy Spirit is "the most honorable of all the beings brought into existence through the Word, the chief in rank of all the beings originated by the Father through Christ." (*On John,* 2,6; *PG*14,127ff) Against the modalists he affirms that the Three are numerically distinguishable, and not verbally only. To call them one in essence and one in subsistence is wrong: as subsistents they are not one but Three.

ORIGEN: THE SUBORDINATIONIST STREAM   Sometimes Origen describes the unity of the Three as if they existed in a moral union only, or in the harmony provided by a virtually identical will. To illustrate the relation of the persons he uses the analogies of the married who are two in one flesh and the justified man who has the same spirit as Christ. He is saved from Tertullian's *separatio* by the notion that the Son and the Spirit derive their being in its entirety from the Father, and that the godhead they possess wells forth from his essence. His use of the term "secondary God" for the Son is therefore an attempt to describe an eternal coming forth and not a lesser condition. The Son is an effluence of the Father, he says, citing Wisdom 7,25 in a pattern of biblical use common to all the Fathers; hence why is he not *homooúsios*, of one substance with that body of which he is a vapor? As brightness comes from light and steam from water, so the Son in coming from the Father, who alone is God strictly, has an identity of divine essence with him even if it is derived.

It is almost impossible to clear Origen of the charge of subordinationism of the Son, much less a tendency to it. His description of Christ as meriting a secondary degree of honor after the God of all things certainly accounts for the charge that he authored a whole subordinationist tradition. He calls the Son the Father's minister, using the term that describes "servants of the word" in St. Luke's prologue. In the work of creating the Son does an errand for the Father—an idea found in Irenaeus. Origen outlaws prayer to Christ directly, saying that any that is offered to him he must convey to the Father. In this he differs from Clement of Alexandria who says we pray to both because they are one and the same God. (*The Pedagogue,* 1,8) His most vulnerable point seems to be his claim that the Father is higher above the Son and the Holy Spirit than they are above the world of creatures; so profound is the influence of the Platonic hierarchy of beings on him that he must demand a near abyss after the One. The Father produces all things through his Word. Therefore he produces the Holy Spirit through his Word, the noblest one of all so produced. (*On John, loc. cit.;* PG14,126)

The Search for a Trinitarian Vocabulary

Origen lived out his days not in Alexandria but in Caesarea on the seacoast of Palestine. His influence long remained, however, in the catechetical (actually theological) school which he had headed. Two successive directors there named Theognotus and Pierius who spanned the second half of the third century were faithful to his memory. The first-named called Christ a creature (actually, "product" might be a better translation *[ktisma]* since elsewhere he said Christ's substance came from the Father), and the second spoke of Father and Son as two substances (*ousíai*) or natures (*phýseis*). It should be evident by now that these two terms plus *hypostáseis* and *prósōpa* were all doing duty in the scramble to arrive at the proper word to signify what we now mean by person. A weakness in all but *prósōpa* is that, being the correct philosophical terms for nature, essence, and substance, they connoted a triplicity of Gods to the unfriendly ear. *Prósōpa* on the other hand could be declared a transitory form or aspect, hence Sabellian. As to the use of "creature," since St. Gregory the Wonderworker (d. after 270) employs both it and *poíēma*—something made or fashioned—while elsewhere calling Jesus "God from God" and saying that in the Triad there is nothing created, it seems that he is merely describing the subsistence of the Son as coming from the Father.

The Two Dionysiuses

A classic case of the tangle caused by words that stood for different emphases occurred in an exchange of letters between the bishops of Alexandria and Rome, both named Dionysius, in the middle of the third century. The former was Origen's pupil. He very unwisely tried to put down a Sabellian outbreak in his jurisdiction by a letter which he addressed to two of the bishops concerned. They reported to Rome that he had distinguished between the Father and Son to the point of separating the two, even naming one without the other as if they were divisible; that he had failed to call the Son *homooúsios* with the Father; had described him as a *poíēma* of God and one who was *genētón* (see p. 59 below); said he was as distinct from the Father according to *ousía* as a boat is from its maker; lastly, that he had denied the Son's eternity by saying that the Father had not always been Father and that "the Son was not before he came into existence." We have left those terms in Greek because the moment we supply English equivalents we take a stand on the Alexandrian bishop's meaning, and that is something we cannot be absolutely sure of.

Starting with the last phrase: if he really said it (and we have only St. Athanasius' report from a century later that he did), then he was a genuine pre-Arian. The statement that "the Son was not before he came into existence" is so redolent of the controversies of the first quarter of the fourth century, however, that one wonders whether Dionysius might

49

have simply repeated the familiar, Platonic-sounding idea that the Son was not Son before he became such immediately prior to the creation. Pursuing this line further, suppose Dionysius meant by *poíēma* a deed of God and by *genētón* one begotten, in other words by neither term signifying "creature." He would probably have meant individual person by *ousía*, not the divine substance, being a pupil of Origen; and if he took *homooúsios* to mean "the same person as" the Father he would have quite rightly rejected it as a modalist term.

None of this is done to exonerate the zealous bishop by forcibly rendering him orthodox. It is used merely as a helpful device to understand the East-West differences of thought and language just before the Arian storm broke. At that time it became clear that when pressed Arius meant the Son of God to be a creature in the strict sense. In the century preceding, it was by no means so evident that those in the Origenist tradition had any such intent. They were struggling to find the right word for a distinct divine person. Their choice, *ousía*, lost out to *hypóstasis*, for no compelling intrinsic reason. *Hypo-stasis*, it is well to recall, is rendered exactly in Latin by *sub-stantia*, and Tertullian had used this term for the reality of the godhead itself. They were also trying to express what we now call the eternal generation of the Son. Tragically, almost everything they chose to express the ideas "begotten," "produced," or "sent forth" had a ring of less-than-full-divinity about it, when all they wished to say was logically-after-therefore-other-than-Father.

To return to the Dionysian unpleasantness, the pope produced a letter on the subject, which was not addressed directly to his brother bishop. The former was shocked at the teaching of three *hypostáseis* (the word for person that did win out) because it connoted three powers or divinities. God is never without his Word and his Spirit who must ever be gathered up into him. The Son originated not by an act of creation—it would be blasphemous to say so—but by a "divine and indescribable generation." Pope Dionysius' expression of orthodoxy, in the spirit of Novatian, won from the Alexandrian teacher a tacit admission that he had gone overboard in his anti-Sabellian zeal. He answered in much more careful language, though without making any admissions of faulty doctrine. First of all, he said, the terms Father and Son imply one another, and Spirit implies both the Source from which and the Medium through which he proceeds. Nonetheless, if we cannot say "three *hypostáseis*" we threaten to dissolve the inseparable Triad. As to *homooúsious*, although it is unscriptural it is admissible since we use similar terms to describe the likeness of parents and children, a river and its source, a plant and its root.

This admission of Dionysius of Alexandria of the term's legitimacy highlights the ambivalence that marked it and would mark it even after Nicaea accepted it. To the West it meant someone identical in *ousía* or substance whereas the East largely viewed it as denoting an individual identical in all respects—even, it would seem, a member of a genus, to the Origenist school. The latter notion is, of course, unacceptable since the deity is neither a genus in three species nor a species with three members. Perhaps sensing the weakness of his analogies rooted in genus and species, Dionysius concluded his response to the pope in a concessive tone: "We both expand the Monad into the Triad without dividing it, and again we sum up the Triad in the Monad without subtracting from it." This statement is fully in accord with the Western spirit of unity of substance yet sufficiently Plotinian to satisfy an Alexandrian. It would not do as a formula, however, to resolve intellectual tensions that went much deeper. Both East and West still had to face the problem of the terms in which to describe the three persons, their relation to the one divine substance, and their relations among themselves.

The differences between East and West were far from being merely terminological. As Sydney Smith said of the two bickering housewives in their back gardens, they could never come to agreement because they were arguing from different premises.

"The Son who is the effulgence of the Father's splen-
dour and the stamp of God's very being." (Heb
1,3) . . . " For the divine nature was his from the first;
yet he did not think to snatch at equality with God, but
made himself nothing, assuming the nature of a slave."
(Phil 2, 6) (Italian sculpture of the fifteenth century;
private collection, Zürich; courtesy *Jubilee* magazine)

CHAPTER THREE

THE ARIAN CRISIS
AND AFTER

We saw in the last chapter that the third-century teacher Paul of Samosata was a trinitarian heretic only in virtue of the adoptionist Christology which was his main concern. The question of who Christ was in relation to the Father proved to be the key one in the storm that broke in the early third century. The Church's mute need for clarification of the mystery of the One and the Three came through the circumstance of a basic denial of a tenet of Catholic faith by a priest of Alexandria named Arius. For a while it seemed that he merely suffered from the linguistic imprecisions of his age and wished to profess Catholicity at all costs. His opponents appeared the ignorant ones in the early stages, unequal to the subtleties of Origen's theology. Arius was also shielded in the early stages by a political situation in which Constantine seemed to want harmony between Church and Empire above all, and to be quite willing to suppress theological wrangles through a council of his own convening to achieve it. In the event, it was established that no matter what the political confusions of the times and the basic Western inability to see the East's point about the meaning of the fluid term *homooúsios*, Arius was a heretic. He was the heretic the Church "needed," so to say, to explicitate her faith in the Father-Son relation and ultimately to take a stand on what Trinitarian orthodoxy consisted in.

Arius began to write about the nature of the Word in 318, as a member of a group of extremist theologians who were in the tradition of Origen. Alexander was bishop of Alexandria at the time (313–28). He is best known perhaps as the predecessor in that office of St. Athanasius, who accompanied him to the Council of Nicaea in the role of secretary. The chief contention of Arius was that God alone is unbegotten (*agénē-tos*), or put conversely, only that which is unbegotten is God. He alone is without beginning (*ánarchōs*). As to the second term, none would have disputed him, but the question immediately arose, did he mean by the first one, uncreated (for this God is uniquely), or unbegotten as well? The proper Greek word for unoriginated, self-existent, is *agénnētos* with two "n's." As soon as Arius intimated that the only one who is God is he who is unbegotten (and the transition from *genētós* to *gennētós* to describe Christ—"begotten" to "created"—was easy), he had denied divine status to the Son, for in Catholic faith the Son is uncreated but begotten. "Without beginning" is a synonym for unoriginated; it is not a synonym for unbegotten. By a calculated confusion, therefore, Arius meant "unoriginated" to include "unbegotten."

THE ARIAN ASSUMPTIONS

Arius held that it was impossible for the godhead (the divine *ousía*, essence) to be communicated or shared with another. If it were, this would mean divisibility, change in God. There was no creature so exalted that God could achieve this transfer of his substance to him. Any participation in God the Father by another would mean that there were two Gods. By inexorable logic, therefore, the Word was a creature for Arius, someone made from nothing. If Catholics say that the Father "begot" him they must mean "made him to be." If you call the Word the portion, emanation, effluence of God, and do not mean to be engaging in mere illustrative speech, you have applied unthinkable categories to God.

The Arian position on the Son was that he was a perfect creature. It was quite fitting to bestow on him the title of God as a courtesy, since he was that first work of God through whom the Father accomplished all the rest. Despite the Word's essential contingency and his own beginning, he is the creator of time born outside time. Arius devised a watchword to describe the Son's generation: "There was when he was not," which cleverly omitted all mention of time. The Son can not have direct knowledge of the Father, for although he is God's Word and Wisdom he is such by participation—not the essential Word and Wisdom of God. He is dissimilar to God as creatures are; he is changeable, even capable of sin (though in practice most Arians held that God had providentially confirmed him in grace); he is, puzzlingly, a member of a holy Triad of three *hypostáseis*. On examination, the latter prove to be God and his chief two creatures.

Arius' method of theological argument was biblical even though his inspiration may have been Plotinian. He pressed all the sap out of Old Testament texts in which wisdom was either a creature or a divine attribute. In the New Testament his favorites were "The Father is greater than I" (Jn 14,28) plus any in which Jesus is established as Lord and Christ or enthroned for having completed the work of salvation. (Ac 2,36; Rom 8,29; Col 1,15; Heb 3,2) In a word, Arius made a demigod of him, one worthy of all honors short of divine. He claimed throughout to be no more than a disciple of a certain Lucian who had been martyred at Antioch in 312. Eusebius of Nicomedia was a theological ally; so was Bishop Eusebius of Caesarea, the historian, who took him in after his condemnation and lived to regret it. The latter was no theologian but probably no heretic either—rather an Origenist subordinationist who resented what he thought was the power-play of Constantine in league with Western theology to attain a political end.

THE POLITICAL DIMENSION

Constantine had been seated on the imperial throne in the West since the death of his father, Constantius Chlorus, in 306. The latter had worshipped *Sol Invictus,* the unconquerable sun. One of the early acts of the young Constantine was to strike Jupiter and Hercules from the Roman coins and put the single sun god in their place. In 311, on the eve of his military triumph at the Milvian bridge, Constantine invoked in a panegyric "the divine spirit that governs this world." He became a Christian, in his broad sympathies, at the time of this victory which made him supreme in the West. His background was thoroughly "monarchian," however, and it is impossible to know what he thought of the person of Christ. We are certain that he never became so much as a catechumen, and that he was baptized on his deathbed (337).

It should therefore not surprise us that the Arian interpretation of faith in the godhead proved attractive to him—not to speak of the political attractiveness of aligning himself from distant Rome with the bulk of the Egyptian clergy, Rome where he became sole ruler upon Licinius' death in 324.

The decades before and after Constantine's decree of political liberty for Christians (Edict of Milan, 313) were marked by a bitter schism in the Alexandrian church. Those who, from the time of persecution under the emperor Diocletian (303), had identified authentic Catholicity with perfect fidelity to Christ under the stress of persecution were to become known as the Donatists. This party of puritan rigorism included in its ranks a certain Meletius of Alexandria who went into schism, consecrating and ordaining men of the stricter view. Arius, as we have already mentioned, had been a "Meletian" cleric, but Bishop Alexander, upon his accession in 313, had received him back into communion and given him a large church in the Baucalis district. In 318 Arius published his views in *Thalia* ("The Banquet"), a symposium of prose and verse. The only fragments of it that remain are found in Athanasius' writings. The response of Arius' bishop was to call a synod in which he was formally excommunicated by a vote of 98 to 2, after fruitless attempts at mediation by Constantine's friend, Hosius of Córdoba.

56   Alexander, remember, was an Origenist, like all the Alexandrians, but a moderate one. He was no Sabellian, surely (as Arius accused him

of being for insisting on the unity of the Triad). For him the Father alone was unoriginate—*agénnētos*. The Word was a distinct person (*hypóstasis*) or nature (*phýsis*), by which Alexander quite evidently meant an individual other than the Father. The Word was no creature but One derived from the Father's being who mediated with creation. The Son as Son was coeternal with the Father, his Image who was always with him, a real and natural Son as opposed to an adoptive one. (Cf. *Letter to Alexander of Byzantium*, 26f, in Theoderet, *Ecclesiastical History*, 1,4.) Like Origen, Alexander taught an eternal generation (*ánarchos génnēsis*) of the Son from the Father. They are "two realities inseparable from one another"; between them there is a "perfect likeness."

THE FAITH OF ARIUS

We possess a record of the faith of Alexander from his response to the teaching of his priest Arius. The earliest account of Arius' belief is contained in a profession of faith (*Ékthesis Písteōs*) submitted to Alexander in 320 by a group which included, among others, Eusebius of Nicomedia. In part, it said: "We acknowledge one God, who is alone unoriginate (*agénnēton,* meaning to them also unbegotten), alone eternal, alone without beginning (*ánarchon*), alone true, alone sovereign, alone judge of all." (Athanasius, *On Synods*, 16; cf. also Hilary *On the Trinity*, 4,12f; 6,5f.) The God here spoken of is the Father. He is indivisible and not subject to any change; hence to speak of his unique being or essense (*ousía*) as capable of communication is unthinkable. Any other beings who exist must have come into existence. Participation in the divine nature means a duality of divine beings if it means anything.

Such was the teaching of Arius that brought him excommunication. He was even more explicit in writing to Bishop Eusebius of Nicomedia—influential with Constantine through friendship with his sister Constantia, who was Licinius' wife, in achieving his reinstatement. Arius wrote him, in 321, "in the interests of that all-conquering truth which you also champion":

> I thought it my duty . . . to advise you . . . how grievously the bishop [Alexander] attacks and persecutes us . . . [and] drives us from the city as atheists because we do not concur with him when he publicly preaches, "God [has] always been, the Son [has] always

[been]; as the Father is, so the Son is; the Son coexists with God, un-originate; he is always being begotten without having been originated by begetting; neither by thought nor by any interval of time does God precede the Son; God always is, the Son always is; the Son proceeds from God himself. (Theoderet, *Ecclesiastical History,* I,5,1–4)

Arius then lamented the condemnation of six Eastern bishops, including Eusebius of Caesarea, who had simply taught, like the Eusebius of Nico-media who received this letter, that "God existed, without beginning, before the Son." He rightly stigmatized as heretical any teaching that called the Son an effluence or projection, or that described him as co-unbegotten.

But what we say and think we both have taught and continue to teach; that the Son is not unbegotten, nor part of the unbegotten in any way, nor is he derived from any substance; but that by his own will and counsel he existed before times and ages fully God, only-begotten, unchangeable. (*Ibid.*)

Little objection can be raised against the Catholicity of the above teach-ing. Arius continued:

And before he was begotten or created or appointed or established he did not exist; for he was not unbegotten. We are persecuted because we say that the Son has a beginning, but God is without beginning. For that reason we are persecuted and because we say he is from noth-ing [what is not]. And this we say because he is neither part of God, nor derived from any substance. For this we are persecuted; the rest you know. (*Ibid.*)

It was in concluding this letter, written from Caesarea in Palestine where Arius had sought refuge, that he linked the name of Eusebius with his own as a fellow-disciple of Lucian of Antioch: both were *"Syl-loukianístoi."*

THE ARIAN SYLLOGISM

This communication was written after his exposition of faith (*Ék-thesis*) addressed to his own bishop, in which the famous "Arian syllo-gism" appears. As the Church historian Socrates reports the latter (ca.

58

440), Arius responded to the Sabellianism he thought he detected in Alexander's teaching by saying:

> If the Father begot the Son, he that was begotten had a beginning of existence; hence it is clear that there was [a time] when he was not. It follows then of necessity that he had his existence from the non-existent. (Socrates, *Ecclesiastical History*, 1,5; cf. M. J. Rouet de Journel, *Enchiridion Patristicum*, 648–51, for documentation on Arius.)

Arianism can be seen as a system of logic which flows from the assumption that the Father, in being self-existent, unoriginated (*agénnētos*), and unbegotten (*agénētos*), is therefore opposed in his deity not only to all who are originated (by his creating them), but also to all who may be begotten from him (as the Son is). The Word is quite simply a creature and a product (*ktísma kai poíēma*); when he is called God it is only in virtue of a metaphorical usage (*katachrestikōs*). Arius thought that a son coeternal with the Father would make two self-existent principles, hence bring an end to monotheism.

THE COUNCIL OF NICAEA

The Alexandrian synod of 318 had not brought a settlement of the Arian question; Arius had subsequently received the support of councils of bishops at Nicomedia and Caesarea. In 325 the emperor called a council to decide the matter, and also to decide the date of Easter. We know the names of over 220 of those in attendance; an allegory puts the number of the council fathers at 318. (Cf. Gn 14,14.) Greece, Egypt, and Asia were well represented; from the West there came but five, two of them representing the aged Pope Sylvester. Hosius was in attendance, the Spanish prelate who resided in Constantine's household.

The sessions met from May 20 to July 25, 325. Constantine addressed the meeting early, in Latin (he had brought the delegates there with imperial funds), then withdrew in favor of "the council's leaders," whoever they might have been. Arius' position had been weakened somewhat by a vote of 53 to 3 against him in a synod held at Antioch in January of that year. The extensive letter-writing campaign of Bishop Alexander during the enforced absence of Arius from his see had evidently borne fruit. Constantine joined to the theological vulnerability of Arius his own

59

plea for a peaceful assembly, saying that the sight of "sedition" within the Church caused him more concern than any battle.

We do not have a record of the acts of the council, but a letter of condemnation of Arius is extant. All but two bishops signed it; these were excommunicated and banished with Arius. The creed says in part that,

> examination was made into the impiety and lawlessness of Arius and his followers, in the presence of our most God-beloved sovereign Constantine, and it was unanimously decided that his impious opinion should be anathematized, together with all the blasphemous sayings and expressions which he has uttered . . . affirming that "the Son of God is from what is not" and "there was [a time] when he was not"; saying also that the Son of God, in virtue of his free-will, is capable of evil and good, and calling him a creature and a work. All these utterances the holy Synod anathematized. . . . (Socrates, *Ecclesiastical History,* 1,9)

Reports had it that twenty-two (or seventeen) of the bishops were sympathetic to the Arian position. How much of the unanimity is attributable to the influence of the emperor's confidant Hosius we do not know. As to the creed adopted by Nicaea, the suggestion was first made by Eusebius of Caesarea that the formula of belief of his church be chosen. It was perfectly orthodox, but its phrases about the Son, "only-begotten, firstborn of all creation, begotten of the Father before all ages," did not meet the Arian position. It served as the basis of Nicaea's creed, however. The latter contained the additional phrases "of the substance [*ousía*] of the Father . . . true God of true God, begotten not made, of one substance with the Father [*homooúsion tōi patri*] . . . who . . . came down . . . and became man [*enanthrōpēsanta*]." At its close the creed says in an appendix that the Catholic and Apostolic Church anathematizes those who hold " 'There was when he was not,' and 'Before he was begotten he was not,' or those who allege that the Son of God is 'Of another substance or essence,' or 'created,' or 'changeable,' or 'alterable.' " (Cf. D 54[126], June 19, 325.)

The Fathers of Nicaea simply reaffirmed the faith witnessed to by Scripture and non-scriptural tradition alike that the Word is truly God, hence cannot suffer change. We do not know what reasons they alleged. Probably they warned against a Triad made up of God and two creatures, or pointed out as Athanasius was later to do that unless Christ is God our

60

redemption is a sham, since the divinity of the Word is essential to the "congruity" of the mediation achieved by Christ the Lord.

By saying that the Son was of the Father's substance (*ousía*, i.e. essence, innermost being, God-ness), Nicaea chose against this meaning for *hypóstasis* and anticipated the usage which Basil and the two Gregorys would stabilize, namely *hypóstasis* for person or individual and *ousía* for substance.

As to *homooúsion*, the term was Constantine's express choice. Its unscriptural nature handicapped it badly, not to speak of its Sabellian connotations. Eusebius of Caesarea—quite unhappy with the term—wrote home to his church that it meant that the Son bore no resemblance to creatures but was in every respect like the Father and came from him, "not from any other *hypóstasis* or *ousía*." He also provided a few explanations of the definition that were neither distinctively Arian nor Catholic.

HOMOOÚSIOS ACCORDING TO NICAEA

What, actually, did the fathers of the Council mean by this Greek term which we translate "consubstantial"? There can be no doubt that they intended to describe a real or metaphysical sonship, but how? The Son derives his being from the Father and possesses the same divine nature, but in what sense is he *homooúsios*? Total likeness of persons who are numerically two appears to be the intention of the majority at Nicaea, rather than a single substance that is fully possessed by Two. The latter came to be—indeed, probably always was—the Western understanding of the term. There was no readiness whatever for this idea in the East, however. This leads us to suppose that the formula was framed by Westerners (Hosius, says Athanasius) in one sense, while agreed to by Origenists in another. It should be pointed out, however, that Origen could teach that *homooúsios* was as proper to Father and Son as it was to light and brightness or river and stream. (*Fragment on Hebrews, PG*14, 1308)

Ultimately, since the divine substance is one, the persons who possess it must be the one, identical substance. The interpretation of subsequent theologians of the meaning of *consubstantialem Patri* may have been the meaning of the small group that framed the creed of Nicaea; but until then, numerical identity of substance had not been indicated —rather a community of substance possessed by two (or three) persons of the same order. The word was used in the sense of "homogeneous" 61 or "of the same nature" as early as 268 at Antioch. It very probably connoted to most of the signers that the Son was fully God for the reason that he possessed the same divine nature as his Father. Even Arius felt no embarrassment in using *homooúsios* as a word proper to the uniqueness of the godhead. Since the Son's coeternity with the Father is what he, in fact, denied, the council in using the term to affirm it must have had in mind its fittingness to describe generic unity.

THE AFTERMATH OF THE COUNCIL:
DEDICATION, LONG-LINED CREEDS; SIRMIUM

The creed of Nicaea proved to be providential in the long run, but in the decades immediately following promulgation its phrases were attacked as novel, unscriptural, and even metaphysically erroneous. This was chiefly true of "begotten of the Father's substance" and "consubstantial with the Father." Most of St. Athanasius' adventures in being deposed and restored to his see of Alexandria hinged on the non-acceptability of the phrasing. This is another way of saying that if the Arians were actively displeased the Catholics were, by and large, no better pleased.

An assembly of ninety bishops at the dedication of Constantine's "Golden Church" in 341 served as the occasion for a "Dedication Creed" intended as an improvement on that of 325. It contained the phrase "whole from whole" to meet the difficulty that "begotten of the substance of the Father" connoted the partition of materiality to some. Also, there were phrases that could bear an Arian meaning as well as a Catholic, like "image . . . of the substance . . . of the Father" and "firstborn of all creation" coupled with stress on Christ's humanity; it used several other Arian-favored texts (e.g. "I came down from heaven not to do my own will but the will of him who sent me"). Athanasius' treatise *On Synods,* 23 (*PG*26,721) contains the "Dedication Creed." It was a work of conservatives, the middle party trying to conciliate between Arians and Nicaeans.

This basically anti-Sabellian formulation championed the distinction of the three persons, separate in rank and glory, unequivocally, but ended by declaring in a phrase that Arians would surely allow, "If anyone says that the Son is a creature *as one of the creatures, or an offspring as one of the offspring, a work as one of the works,* let him be anathema."

62

Very soon after, Arian sympathizers (Arius had died in 336) made a shorter version of this creed their own. At Sardica (modern Sofia) in 343, however, Western bishops supported Athanasius and the Nicaean formula of 325. A moderate formulation was drawn up at Antioch in 344, the so-called "Long-lined Creed" (*Ékthesis makróstichos*), a wordy compromise which omitted the terms *ousía, hypóstasis,* and *homooúsios* and called the Son—one of three *prósōpa*—"perfect and true God in nature." (Cf. J.N.D. Kelly, *Early Christian Creeds,* pp. 279f.)

Sirmium witnessed in 357 a thoroughly Arian creed which rejected both *homooúsios* and *homoioúsios* (of *same,* and of *like,* substance) as beyond man's grasp, and nonbiblical besides. "There is no doubt that the Father is greater . . . than the Son," it said, "in honor, renown, and deity and in the very name of Father, for the Son himself testifies 'He that sent me is greater than I' (Jn 14,28)." The Son is subject to the Father, together with all the things that the Father has subjected to himself. (Cf. Socrates, *Eccl. Hist.,* 2,30.) Hilary of Poitiers stigmatized this statement as a blasphemy and the name stuck. The "Blasphemy of Sirmium," somewhat like the "Defenestration of Prague," is better known as an event that took place there than as the Arian-oriented creed which in fact it was.

A new term emerged from Sirmium, namely Anomoeism, from the contention of some of the "new Arians" that the Son was unlike (*anómoios*) the Father. Aetius and Eunomius, proponents of this view, argued subtly that the divine *essence* was in no way communicable, but the divine *activity* was. The Son who resulted from this activity, being begotten, must have been "from a different essence" from the Father, whose essence it is to be unbegotten. This teaching granted a conferral on the Word of divinity at the time of his generation, in the sense that a share in the Father's creative power and activity was given him. The Anomoeists eliminated mystery from the Father-Son relation by stating that we can know as much as God can know about his own essence, perfect in its simplicity.

HOMOEANS AND HOMOEOUSIANS—
ARIANS AND CONSERVATIVES

The fifty-odd years between Nicaea and the Council of Constantinople (381) which drew the curtain on the major trinitarian disputes saw the rise of a compromise spirit later to be known as Semi-Arianism.

So, at least, Epiphanius described its adherents a century after. (*Heresies*, 73) Rather than being unquestionably tinged with heresy, as the name might indicate, these were men who were Catholic in sentiment and conservative in terminology; they wished to depart from anti-Nicaeanism, once they saw how many out-and-out Arian heretics marched under the banner of opposition to the creed of 325.

St. Cyril of Jerusalem was a man of this persuasion. It is not uncommon to hear this great pastoral figure spoken of as if he were "soft on Arianism," whereas like so many of his time his scruples were only against the wording of Nicaea. When he spoke of the Son as "like the Father in all things" (*homoioúsios*), he was not describing the similarity of creature to Creator but the likeness of Two who, because they have the same will and operation, are equally God. (Cf. *Catechetical Lectures*, 4,7; 6,6; 11,16.) Bishop Basil of Ancyra—modern Ankara, the capital of Turkey—rallied these forces at a synod in 358; the term Homoeousian emerged from the decrees which it issued. (Cf. Epiphanius, *Heresies*, 73,3–11.) A certain subordinationist strain is not entirely absent, taking the form of the view that the Son's generation is a result of the Father's free will. Still, this notion is to be found, verbally at least, in the writings of Athanasius and Hilary. The Ancyra synod was firmly anti-Arian at all the strategic points. It used *ousía* in the sense of person for Father and Son. The Two were alike not by identity (*tautótēs*) but by likeness of *ousía*. Ancyra condemned anyone who would use *homooúsios tautoúsios* of the Son and the Father (because of the Sabellian ring to a word not yet unmistakably Catholic after three decades, and particularly its modifier).

Sirmium had rejected *homoioúsios* a year before; now Ancyra espoused it. A year later (359) George of Laodicea spelled out the Homoeousian position, calling for two *hypostáseis* identical "with respect to substance." Father and Son are "like in spirit" or "the same," the one having begotten the other. (Cf. Epiphanius, *ibid.*, 73, 12–22.) The genuine heretics of the mid-fourth century were the Homoeans (Council of Nikē, 359), whose *homoíos*, as applied to Christ, clearly meant to make him a creature who bore a moral resemblance to the Father. If "Semi-Arian" is to be used with any accuracy it should be applied to the Homoeans like Ursacius and Valens at Nikē, not the Homoeousians. Acacius of Caesarea was their leader and the framer of the "Dated Creed" of 359, from its preface, which naively stated that, "The Catholic faith was published . . . on May 22." (Cf. Henry Bettenson, *Documents of The Christian*

64

Church, pp. 61 ff.) It is Catholic in all respects until the end, when in outlawing *ousía* from all religious discussion forever (as too technical, unscriptural) it concludes: "We say that the Son is like the Father [in all things], as the Holy Scriptures say and teach." (Cf. Athanasius *On Synods,* 8.) The bracketed phrase was omitted in the West on an Arian principle, so that when it was promulgated at a council in Constantinople in 360 its meaning was unmistakable. This decree elicited St. Jerome's famous hyperbole, "The world groaned and found itself Arian." (*Dialogue against Lucifer,* 19)

In between Nikē and Constantinople there were held two synods, at Rimini in Italy and Seleucia in Asia Minor, both in 359. Athanasius' *On Synods* is actually about these two, the first of which was Nicaean in spirit, the second Homoean. He points out that endless synods and decrees are an Arian stratagem—not unlike Communist peace negotiations, we might observe.

The activity of Basil of Ancyra meant the turning of the tide, however. From 362—when Athanasius was restored to Constantinople—until 381, a gradual conversion of the moderates was effected. They became men of Nicaean faith and terminology through Basil's compromise formula "like in all things, including *ousía,*" which neither Athanasius nor his Western counterpart St. Hilary of Poitiers hesitated to use.

THE CONTRIBUTIONS OF ATHANASIUS AND HILARY

If the reader thinks that mental laziness on the writer's part accounts for the failure to assign an English meaning to Greek terms as they occur, he is quite wrong. In theological writing, the facile rendering of terms that kept men of good will apart for decades has tended to make the fourth-century disputes all but incomprehensible. It was of the essence of these disputes that there was no agreement on terms—that there was even diametric opposition. There was at the same time the clear intent of some to profess Catholic or trinitarian faith, and of others Arian or unitarian faith. The careers of Athanasius and Hilary are a study of the gradual coincidence of faith and terminology. This development required, however, the residence of Athanasius in Trier and Rome, through two successive banishments from his see (335–346; there were five in all), and the exile of Hilary to Asia Minor in 356–359. Each learned in exile something of how differently East and West viewed Catholic faith

65

while holding unequivocally to its substance. Each also learned from bitter personal experience the large part imperial ambition and episcopal hope of preferment played in the struggle.

Writing in 359, St. Athanasius produced his tract *On Synods* quoted above. In it, this firm Nicaean attempted a reconciliation with the Homoeousians by approaching them peacefully ("as brothers with brothers," 41) yet making the case for *homooúsios* as the only satisfactory term against any Arian wedge. (53f) He can see why "like" can mean "like by participation" in every case but one—when the "likeness" is that of consubstantiality or coessentiality. The word *homooúsios* can have no meaning, says Athanasius, but like-in-substance, like-in-essence. Since the Homoeousians already admit that the Son is "from the Father's *ousía* and not other in *hypóstasis*," that is, a substance alien to divinity, they should have no trouble taking the Nicaean steps. They ought to be able to speak of "identity" of Son with Father rather than "likeness," he holds, thereby staving off any Arian threat.

Hilary attempts a similar irenic approach in his letter of 359 *On Synods*. As he concludes three years in exile he writes to his Western brother bishops summarizing the teaching of Sirmium and Ancyra. In general he is clarifying the distinction between heresy and Catholic faith, but because of Western ignorance of the nature of the Eastern struggle he shows how terms unacceptable in the West can bear a Catholic meaning. Defending *homoioúsios* obliquely, he shows that really-like *can* mean really-equal. (72–75) Then, however, he addresses himself to the bishops of the East and ironically shows that whereas the consciences of some balk at the term *homooúsios* as unscriptural, they can allow the equally unscriptural *homoioúsios* should Arianism or subordinationism be intended. (77–82) Basically Hilary favors the notion of unity of substance (*On the Trinity*, 4,33; 7,33) but he does see the Homoeousian point that the Son's generation from the Father's substance renders him "perfectly like," that is, equal.

The Arian emperor Constantius died in 361, to be succeeded by the anti-Christian Julian. During a brief eight-month interval from exile, Athanasius summoned a council at Alexandria (362). Its acts are available in the brief *Statement to the Church of Antioch*. In it Athanasius puts forth his belief in three *hypostáseis*, making clear that nothing could be farther from his mind than three alien substances. (*Ibid.*, 5) He can even accept one *hypóstasis* if it means to the speaker divine substance. (*Ibid.*, 6) He wants it clear that unity in belief is paramount, whether

66

unity in terminology can be achieved or not. This conciliatory spirit, though it shocked men on both sides as "flabby" (connoting tritheism to the West, modalism to the East), paved the way for the formula of Basil and the two Gregorys that was to win out in East and West: "one nature (*ousía*) in three persons (*hypostáseis*)."

In reading the theological argumentation of Athanasius and Hilary, one is struck by its vigor, bordering on vituperation, and its profoundly biblical character. Both favor the Nicaean settlement for the reason not that its wording is subtle or philosophically apt, but that it stands for the biblical data best. Typology is so firmly entrenched in the thought of the period that arguments for the Trinity from Genesis and Judges are put forward as readily as from the gospels or Paul's letters. Arians, Catholics, and all in between use the same texts in the same way; no one questions the validity of his own exegetical procedure, he simply assumes it. The effect is strange, especially when an argument favoring Christ's eternal generation is framed from a piece of Old Testament wisdom literature with the same apparent certitude as when it is done from the Johannine discourse at the last supper. Certain texts are favorites of one side or the other; for example, "The Father is greater than I" (Jn 14,28) gets much Arian use, whereas "He who sees me sees the Father" (Jn 14,9) receives much treatment at the hands of Catholics. In general, the Arian technique is simply to apply gospel references to Christ's humanity, with all its limitations, to the eternal Logos.

The judgment of any reader of Athanasius's tract *Against the Arians* or Hilary's *On the Trinity* will necessarily be that Catholic preconceptions mark the entire approach to Scripture. The interpretation of every text in the light of the "analogy of faith" comes through very clearly. From boyhood these believers have known of the full divine status of the eternal Son and Spirit. It is not strange that they find it testified to on every page of Scripture. "Let his name be blessed forevermore; his name continues before the sun" (Ps 71[72],17), for example, provides Athanasius with testimony to the worship of the eternal Word. (*Against the Arians*, 1,11,41)

THE FULL DIVINITY OF THE SPIRIT

The Holy Spirit has been largely absent from these pages until now. His status as a divine person was denied by the Arians, needless to say.

67

They considered him different in substance from the Son, just as the Son was different from the Father. Some believers had a "binitarian" concern only, relegating the Spirit to the status of a divine quality of Father and Son. Still others—the great bulk of Catholics—could say little of the Spirit besides the fact that he was, and was divine. Nicaea's original creed, so far as we can reconstruct it from the writings of Eusebius of Caesarea, ended abruptly: "And in the Holy Spirit."

We first hear of the separate and calculated denial of the Spirit in Athanasius's writings when he responds to Bishop Serapion of Thmuis concerning the teaching of the *"trópikoi"* (*trópos*, figure; hence allegorists). They considered the Holy Spirit a creature, an angel, first in rank among the ministering spirits, necessarily "other in substance" than God. Athanasius teaches in response the Spirit's full divinity with the Father and the Son. (*To Serapion*, 1, *passim*) The Egyptian Christians who deny this have done so because of faulty interpretation of biblical, chiefly Old Testament, texts. The Spirit "belongs to and is one with the godhead which is in the triad." (*Ibid.*, 1,21) The latter is eternal, homogeneous, and indivisible. Since the Spirit belongs to it, he must be consubstantial with Father and Son. Like them he is changeless, ubiquitous, unique. He is the Spirit of the Son, "the vital activity and gift whereby he sanctifies and enlightens." Athanasius argues from effect to cause: since the Spirit makes us holy with the holiness of God by dwelling in us as in a temple (1 Cor. 3,16f), he must be divine. He therefore shares one and the same substance with the Father and Son. "The Father accomplishes all things through the Word in the Holy Spirit," is "Athanasius' way of describing the single divine activity, whether of creation, redemption, or whatever. "If the Son is named, the Father is in the Son, and the Spirit is not outside the Word." In 362 at the council of Alexandria, Athanasius got agreement on the proposition that the Holy Spirit was not a creature but belongs to and is inseparable from the substance of the Father and the Son.

This easy grouping of the Three is anything but novel in Christian usage. Men like Eusebius of Caesarea, tinged with Origen's Plotinian language, did speak, it is true, of the Spirit as "in the third rank" and "third from the Supreme Cause"; they found a place for him in the holy Triad, and said he outstripped all creatures in honor and glory. (*Ecclesiastical Theology*, 3,5,17) This subordinationist tendency—almost emanationist—is absent however from the vigorous catechesis of St. Cyril of Jerusalem. His baptismal-preparation lectures of 348 or 349 name the

Spirit as distinct but unconfusedly one of the divine Three. "The Father gives to the Son," Cyril says, "and the Son communicates to the Holy Spirit." (*Catechetical Lectures,* 16,24) He is "ever-present with the Father and the Son" (17,5), and has the same glory that is theirs. (16,4)

Macedonius, Homoeousian bishop of Constantinople (342–360) who was deposed from office under Arian influence, gave his name some twenty years after his death to the heresy that denied the Holy Spirit's divinity. His connection with the party of the Pneumatomachians ("Spirit-fighters") is tenuous at best. The leader of this group—Macedonians, as they are commonly known—was Eustathius of Sebaste, who taught that the Spirit was "neither God nor one of the others" (Didymus the Blind, *On the Trinity,* 2,8), but in some ambiguous middle condition. His was a familiar logical difficulty, impossible of solution if its premise were true: if the Spirit was neither Father nor Son (the only divine relationship allowed by Scripture), he had to be an unoriginated principle like the Father or the brother of the Son; but both positions were unthinkable.

St. Basil, bishop of Caesarea, Cappadocia (370–79), preached the Holy Spirit's full divinity gradually by putting to his hearers the test proposition of whether he was a creature or not. Since the Spirit was inseparable from the Father and the Son in the creeds he must be considered one along with them, one having "the divine and blessed nature," not put in any inferior class. (*Letter* 125,3) He quotes Origen on "the divinity of the adorable Trinity," improving the clarity of his phrasing somewhat, and remarks, as he finds grace in him here, that he "was not always quite sound in his ideas about the Spirit." (*On the Holy Spirit,* 29,73) St. Gregory of Nyssa holds for the oneness of nature of the three persons; again, he argues backwards from the holiness of the Spirit's works to his divine status. It is St. Gregory of Nazianz who brings an end to tentativeness in the discussion by saying that *the Spirit is God,* consubstantial with the Father, the associate of Christ in the work of redemption. (*Catechetical Discourse,* 31,10; 34,11) He is neither a divine "force" nor a creature. Just as the Old Testament period harbored the revelation of the Father and the New Testament that of the Son, so the life of the Church is marked by the Spirit's indwelling and the progressive revelation of his nature.

The Arians had long accused the Catholics of teaching that the Father had two sons. To counter this, Basil distinguished between origin by a process of being begotten and by being breathed forth from God's mouth. The Spirit's coming forth is in a manner unutterable; he is linked with the one Father through the one Son, receiving all his divine qualities through the latter. (*On the Holy Spirit,* 45,47) Gregory of Nazianz contents himself with the word "proceeds" from (Jn 15,26) but he does not say how this differs from the Son's generation or the Father's unbegotten condition. (Cf. *Catechetical Discourse,* 31,7f.)

The Cappadocian trio is so firmly committed to the *homooúsion* of the Holy Spirit that they cannot be thought guilty of subordinationism (as Origen's follower Eusebius of Caesarea surely was) when they name the Son as an agent in producing the Spirit. It is Gregory of Nyssa who works out the theory of a twofold procession of the Spirit that will prove lasting in the East. The Father alone is cause and the other two are caused, the one directly by the Father, the other, the Holy Spirit, through the mediation of the Son. Hence only the latter is only-begotten. The Spirit comes *out of* the Father, who is source of all, *through* the Son; he proceeds from the Father and receives from the Son; the Son is related to the Spirit as cause to effect. (Cf. *Against Macedonius* 2; 10; 12; 24.) An interesting development, but far from typical, occurs when St. Epiphanius dispenses with the mediatory role of the Word and says that the Spirit "comes out of the same substance of the Father and Son," that he is "out of the Father and the Son." (*The Firmly Anchored Man,* 7,7f) He is "from both, a Spirit derived from spirit, for God is spirit." (*Ibid.,* 70) The omission of the "through" to describe the Spirit's origin from the Son is noteworthy. It is, however, an orthodox mode of expression, and will come to prevail in the West.

At the council of Constantinople (381) the consubstantiality of the Son in the Nicaean sense was reaffirmed, and that of the Holy Spirit subjoined. Athanasian thought prevailed. Quite understandably the three distinct hypostases were to the fore in the East rather than the one divine substance. Despite stress on the individual subsistences of Father, Son, and Spirit, all were believed to possess the godhead equally. God exists simultaneously in three hypostases. His divinity is undivided in distinct persons, each of whom inheres in both of the others. Three hypostases possess an identity of nature (*phýsis*). The Father is he out of whom and toward whom the subsequent persons are reckoned, as Gregory of Nazianz expresses it. It is Basil who is clearest about the coinherence that later came to be called *"perichōrēsis."*

Everything that the Father is is seen in the Son, and everything that the Son is belongs to the Father. The Son in his entirety abides in the Father, and in turn possesses the Father in entirety in himself. Thus the hypostasis of the Son is, so to speak, the form and presentation by which the Father's hypostasis is recognized in the form of the Son. (*Letter* 38,8)

The beginnings of a theology of differentiation among the persons in virtue of origin are here, but before that there came the notion of the analogy of a universal *ousía* (now "substance") realized in three particular hypostases. Somewhat as the concept man is realized in three individuals who are men, so each divine person is distinct from the others in virtue of a peculiar property that is his. For the Father it is fatherhood, for the Son sonship, and for the Holy Spirit the power to sanctify or sanctification (*hagiasmós*). Gregory of Nazianz is more specific than Basil, just paraphrased. He prefers "ingenerateness," "generateness," and "mission" or "procession." The Father imparts his being to the Son and Spirit and in that sense causes them, though there is no notion of true subordinationism here. It is origin (in all cases except that of the Father) and mutual relation that determine personality.

One term that comes into use in the late fourth century is "modes of existence," another, "forms of presentation." The latter, *prósōpa*, is a normal Greek word for persons, but *hypóstasis* is not to be dislodged by it. "God" stands for the divine essence or being, Amphilocius of Iconium argues, whereas the names Father, Son, and Holy Spirit stand for "modes of relation." (Cf. PG 39,112.) This is not a new modalism but an attempt to distinguish between the undifferentiated divine substance and the individuality of each person. The godhead cannot be sundered, yet there must be some way of indicating the distinction of persons. God's activity (*enérgeia*) with respect to us is one, therefore his unity is preserved. All three persons work together to create, sanctify and console man, since all possess the one divine nature fully.

It is important for us in the modern period to see how definitive an argument for the unity of divine substance the unity of man's salvation is. The three persons act together, therefore they are the one, indivisible God. There is no danger of understanding the Cappadocians tritheistically, despite their analogy of a genus thrice realized. They know full well that the godhead is a concrete reality, not a conception, and that all similarity of multiple humanity to it is marked by the flaw that numerical "threeness" in God does nothing to destroy unity of essence. The latter is single and indivisible; all use of numbers gives a false impression of quantity, dimension, etc. This stress on the analogical quality of number in God by Evagrius of Pontus, Gregory of Nyssa, and others inevitably resulted in a corresponding stress on God's unique, simple, and incomposite nature.

THE TRINITY IN ST. AUGUSTINE

St. Hilary, it will be recalled, built on the reflections of Tertullian and Novatian in the West. He grew more at ease in the presence of the East's distinction of persons as he got to know that part of Christendom better, but he still was able to stress (in the spirit adopted by the later Trinity preface) that the Three "are one not in union of person but in unity of substance." (*On the Trinity*, 4,22) Their one will and one operation ensure oneness of divine essence.

A forerunner of St. Augustine is Victorinus, a convert-philosopher whose neo-Platonism allows him to see in God an inner dynamism that results in a created universe outside himself and the begetting of the Word within his being. The threefold activity of a God who is by nature movement (in the philosophical sense) includes *being, living,* and *understanding.* Nothing determines the Father. He is absolute, unconditioned. The Son, however, is that form by which the godhead makes itself known, and in that sense he is determinate. The Father knows himself by his Son, just as we also know him thereby. The Son is the Father's life, the Spirit God's understanding. The Father is silence eloquent, says Victorinus. Christ is his voice; "The Paraclete is the voice of the voice." (*Against Arius*, 3,16)

Existence, Life, Knowledge, is another of his poetic triads. He sees the divine substance as threefold, and as being an endless dynamism of being, proceeding, and returning. The Three exist in each other; their mutual indwelling or "circuminsession" is the more static Western equivalent of the Greek *perichōrēsis.* God expresses himself in the Son, his form or image, but knows himself in the Spirit who thereby perfects the divine being. Victorinus prepares the way for Augustine with the view that the human soul is the best analogue for the triune God. It is, it has life, it comprehends, just as the Father first is, then expresses himself in the Son, and finally realizes the full meaning of godhead in the Spirit who is the bond between Father and Son.

72

St. Augustine's trinitarian teaching is largely contained in his treatise

On the Trinity, composed over twenty years. He accepts Catholic teaching on the coessentiality of the divine Three, their distinctness, their fullness of divinity. Nowhere does he argue the mystery since Catholic faith proposes it. All his effort goes into plumbing its intelligibility. His starting-point is the divine being, not the Father as origin and source. This is an important difference from the attempts of his predecessors. The divine *essentia* is Trinity. *Substantia* Augustine tends to reject as contributing to the notion that the godhead can underlie accidents of any sort, such as the divine attributes. God is himself identical with all the qualities that can be attributed to him.

St. Augustine, in taking the divine essence as his starting point, is surely more influential than he knows in all subsequent teaching of the trinitarian mystery in the West. Not only does he stress oneness rather than threeness (something to be expected because he *is* of the West), but he uses the divine nature as his starting point, not the saving deed of God in Christ. His basic catechesis as we know it from *The First Catechetical Instruction* is biblical; the *rudis* or untutored inquirer must first of all be told the story of man's salvation out of the two testaments of Scripture. Nonetheless, very early in his treatise *On Christian Doctrine,* when he begins to propose norms for the understanding of Scripture, he gives the following as the Church's teaching on the "single Trinity, [which is] a certain supreme reality common to all who enjoy it." The "realities" to be enjoyed are the three persons:

> Thus there are the Father, the Son, and the Holy Spirit, and each is God, and at the same time all are one God: and each of them is a full substance, and at the same time all are one substance. The Father is neither the Son nor the Holy Spirit; the Son is neither the Father nor the Holy Spirit; the Holy Spirit is neither the Father nor the Son. But the Father is the Father uniquely; the Son is the Son uniquely; and the Holy Spirit is the Holy Spirit uniquely. All three have the same eternity, the same immutability, the same majesty, and the same power. In the Father is unity, in the Son equality, and in the Holy Spirit a concord of unity and equality; and these three equalities are all one because of the Father, all equal because of the Son, and all united because of the Holy Spirit. (*On Christian Doctrine* 1,5)

This formula contributes greatly to that theological exposition of the fifth or sixth century known as the Athanasian Creed, *Quicunque vult.* Its viewpoint is ontological; in other words, God is seen in terms of His own eternal inner life. The Father's initiative to save us, the Son's taking 73 flesh, the Spirit's dwelling in our hearts, are all prescinded from or at least assumed to be already known. The paradox is that these divine deeds are presumed known in the very act of framing a principle through which the whole body of Scripture, which contains these deeds, may be examined.

There is no danger of mistaking the unity of the Trinity in Augustine's explanation. He also outlaws completely any subordinationism by his insistence that whatever can be said of any one of the persons can be said of all three. (*On the Trinity*, 5,9) In respect of the divinity no one person is greater than any other, nor is any one less than the Trinity itself. Only as to person is there difference. Augustine will not allow the term *triplex* to describe the mystery because it connotes three individuals to him. (*Ibid.*, 6,9) He likes *Trinitas* because it basically means tri-unity. The notion of the coinhering of the Three in each other saves their unity for him.

If Father, Son, and Spirit are one because each is fully to be identified with the divine substance (they being not individuals of a genus as creatures are), and if the singular number, not the plural, is correct to describe the divine reality ("not three increates, eternals, omnipotents," the *Quicunque* will say, "but one"), then we should expect Augustine to posit a single divine principle of activity. And so he does. Describing the creation of Christ's humanity he declares it done by the Trinity, "for the works of the Trinity are not separable." (*On Faith, Hope, and Charity*, 38) His phrase is that the Three act as "one principle"—in other words, that a single divine essence-will is responsible for all that may be attributed to Father, Son, or Spirit—their individual personalities alone excepted. All that they do inseparably they do outside the divine nature and with respect to contingents.

Augustine provides us here with categories that seem familiar to us because they are our own. He, in fact, gave them to us. But we must understand how much of a departure they represented in his day when the various activities of the godhead were ascribed to this or that person without question, and not to the divine essence. The ascription of the theophanies of the Old Testament to the Son is a case in point. In facing the objection that his theology fails to observe sufficiently the distinction among the divine persons, Augustine answers that all that God does in the temporal order he does in a Trinity of indivisible persons. The Word alone takes flesh, but the Father and Son are by no means inactive in the deed. The Son's death and resurrection by which we are saved is a work,

74

quite simply, of the godhead. Yet in virtue of the Son's eternal relation to the Father there is a certain fittingness that the indivisible will of God should be made manifest through him.

The Bishop of Hippo does not think that when a voice speaks at Jesus' baptism it is the Trinity but the Father speaking. Similarly, the Trinity does not descend in the form of a dove—it is the Spirit; only the Son, not the Trinity, took flesh of Mary, suffered, and rose from the dead. Such is Catholic faith, he says, as is the complementary teaching that when any of the Three acts he acts inseparably since they are inseparable. (On the Trinity, 1,4,7) Along with this fact there is the further fact that no member of the Trinity possesses the divine nature in the same way as the others. Hence there is a certain fittingness in attributing certain works outside of God to certain persons in virtue of their origin. To illustrate: while the visible humanity of Christ is a creature brought into being by an act of the divine will, and while Father, Son, and Spirit are inseparable in the work of the incarnation, to the Son who is sole-begotten of the Father (ibid., 5,6) and co-bestower of the Spirit (ibid., 5,12) is properly attributed the work of redemptive incarnation.

The basis of this attribution must be some distinction among what Latin theology is universally calling the tres personae in Augustine's time. Who are these personae? Three who are somehow individual. Yet as individual existents Augustine cannot accept them. It is only in despair at needing a human word to avoid the modalist error that he agrees to "persons" (ibid., 7,7ff); he is not satisfied, however, until he has worked out his theory that this term actually stands for subsistent relations. Clearly the Three cannot be accidents of the one divine substance. Neither can they be three distinct substances, or they would not be the one God. What remains for Augustine is that they exist as distinct just as surely as the facts of begetting, being begotten, and proceeding (or being bestowed) are eternal realities in the godhead. Books 5 to 7 of his treatise On the Trinity give his solution at length.

The Father is a Father because he is unbegotten, and the Son a Son because he is begotten. No one may call the Spirit a Father since he is not unbegotten nor does he beget anyone. The Spirit is not a second Son for the reason that the Father does not beget him. The notion that the Father and Son together would beget him Augustine finds monstrous. (On The Trinity, 15,26,47) The Spirit proceeds (ekporeúetai) from the Father; Jesus says in the same breath that he will send him (pémpsō) **75** from the Father. (Jn 15,26) He comes upon men as a gift (dōreá, Ac

2,38; 10,45). Except for the last cited New Testament phrase, which describes the outpouring in time of the Spirit's sanctifying action, the remaining biblical data can be taken as describing the persons in terms of mutual relations. The way in which they stand with respect to each other describes their origins one from another. Actively taken this may be procession (*probolē, próbasis*) or, when it is a question of an eternal person resulting from inner action in the godhead, *productio,* in the usage of the Latin fathers. The Father is the chief source. From him the Son comes forth, and the Spirit in common from both. The Father first gives all he has to his Son, including the power to bestow the Spirit. (*On the Trinity,* 15,47)

Anyone who has heard the theological phrase "subsistent relation," though he may not take in its full meaning, at least fails to be struck immediately by any contradictory element. Yet in ordinary experience there is nothing quite of this sort. Two men who are cousins—or who are standing next to each other, or are employer and employee—exist in a mutual relation; this fact, however, by no means accounts for their being as subsistents. The creature *needs* subsistence in order to stand in relation to another. Augustine was less hampered than the modern thinker on this point. The notion was a common philosophical one in his time (cf. Plotinus, *Enneads,* 6,1,6ff), and it aided him immensely in avoiding the seeming contradiction involved in any vocabulary attempt at describing trinity in unity. Father and Son form a single principle with relation to the Spirit because their relation to him (of origin, i.e.) is identical. The operation of two divine persons is inseparable where there is no difference of relation. Hence we find Augustine an early teacher of the double procession of the Spirit from the Father and the Son (the *Filioque* of the later creedal phrase). Why not *per Filium,* the phrase the East leaned toward? Because if Father and Son were *one principle* in respect to the production of the Holy Spirit, it was all one to Augustine how it happened. Their relation to him was identical: hence "and from the Son" described the Spirit's procession as accurately for Hippo's bishop as "through the Son."

St. Augustine's designation of the Holy Spirit as the gift (*donum;* St. Hilary uses the synonym *munus*) which the Father and Son bestow commonly raises the question of whether he can be eternally given if there is no recipient. The Father-Son relation is eternal. Can the Spirit be an eternal gift if he is given to us men and that only in time? Or if not to us, then to whom is he given? Augustine distinguishes: the Holy

Spirit is eternally a *donum,* who is *donatum* only in time. (*On the Trinity,* 5,15,16) He is as it were a consubstantial *communio* of Father and Son (5,27,50), an eternal gift of love who is then poured into our hearts. Being given by, or coming forth from, the Father and Son is what keeps him both from being a creature and from being a Son. He is given, not begotten as the Son is (*non natus sed datus*), and is given to us in the grace of adoption as sons only after he has first been *given* absolutely by Father and Son. (5,14,15) Father and Son have a love in common which is of the same divine substance as they themselves—the Spirit not of one of them but of both. His whole divine being is the result of a giving rooted in a common love, namely, the single will-act of two who are divine. The *donatio* is, in fact, substantial personal Love.

Neither Scripture nor the Greek Fathers describe the Holy Spirit in terms of love. He is for the Greeks "holiness" (St. Gregory the Wonderworker, St. Basil), or "holiness itself" (St. Gregory of Nazianz), doubtless because of the scriptural attribution to him of the work of human holiness. Augustine argues that since Father and Son are spirit, and since both are holy, the Holy Spirit is called such properly because he is the substantial and consubstantial holiness of both. (Cf. R1750.) He also calls the Spirit the unity of Father and Son. It is as their common love or goodness (*caritas, sanctitas, unitas*), however, that Augustine conceives him above all. (Cf. R1665.) Love being an act of will, the stage is set for the later Thomistic development which will see the roots of the person of the Holy Spirit in a certain "impelling and motive force," namely the divine act of will, whereby he proceeds. (*Summa Theologiae* 1,36,1 ad 2) The Spirit is not to be called begotten nor unbegotten, for that would make him a Son or a Father respectively. His eternal beginnings are by way of procession from both, "from the Father principally, and without any interval of time, commonly from both." (*On the Trinity,* 15,26,47) It is from the Father, in other words, that the Son receives the Spirit and hence has any capacity to bestow him.

Augustine's stress on the ideas of "gift" and "love" with respect to the procession of the Holy Spirit is important but it is not what distinguishes him chiefly in the realm of trinitarian theology. He is far better known for his use of analogies to convey the unity of the divine nature and the distinctness of the Three who possess it. He is sympathetic to his predecessors who use the sun's light or a spring's course through a river to a stream to illustrate the mystery. All nature bears the stamp of its Creator in Augustine's view; but since God is Trinity the impress of the 77 divine Three will be found everywhere. The best reflection of God's inner life, naturally enough, is the creature man as crown of the visible universe.

God looked within himself ("Let us . . .") in creating man in his image and likeness. Introspection on man's part yields something of what that likeness is. Even in his life of sense perception man gains some clue to the trinitarian life of God. There is the *object* seen, the internal *image* produced by the object, and the *intention* (or act of focussing) of the mind which binds object and representation together. (*On the Trinity*, 11,2,2) A similar triad but more interior still is comprised by the *memory impression*, the *internal memory image*, and the *setting of the will*. (11,3,6–9) Augustine understandably favors analogies out of man's spiritual or intellectual life rather than his sense life, because God is spirit. The tabular representation below will give some idea of the variety of Augustinian usage:

Father	Son	Holy Spirit
1. Lover	Beloved	Their love
2. Being	Knowing	Willing
3. Being	Understanding	Living
4. Memory (i.e. the mind's latent self-knowledge)	Understanding (i.e. the mind's self-apprehension)	Will (i.e. the mind's self-love)
5. Our remembrance of God	Our knowledge of God	Our love for God
6. Mind	(Self-) Knowledge	(Self-) Love
7. Human genius	Indoctrination	Enjoyment

Early in his career he worked out the being, knowing, willing triad. (*Confessions*, 13,11) Nos. 4,5, and 6 above are subsequent elaborations on it. (*On the Trinity*, 10,17,19; 14,11 to end; 9,2–8) It is generally supposed that the first triad above (No. 1) represented his favorite analogy, but two who are in a relation of love served Augustine merely as a step to considering man's inner life—already a unity—in its triune aspects. He thought that all the examples above from 2 to 7 conveyed the mutual relations among the equal and coordinate elements of human personality, the first on the left being basic to the other two as the Father is in his role of principle of origin. His favorite was number 5 above, a more satisfactory analogy in every way than the one preceding it because the human faculties, although unitary, are not brought to their perfection until they have God as their object. Man, like God, is one substance and not three.

When he is absorbed in his totality—imagery, thought, volition—with the divine Being, then he is most like that Being, who is triune.

Augustine was not deluded concerning the limitations of his various analogies. He points out that no image of God that man may carry about with him is identical with him in the way the Son who is God's image is identical in substance with the Father. Man has a nature which has certain faculties really distinct from it as qualities or modifications. In the Trinity all is simple. Memory, understanding, and will are separate in their operation, but the Trinity is absolutely one and indivisible because its members coinhere. Most paradoxical of all for Augustine, the single notion of the Trinity possessed by the human mind is as nothing in its unity compared with the substantial unity of the Three themselves.

One final consideration concerns Augustine's doctrine of divine missions and theophanies. Only the Father is described in Scripture as not having been sent because he is neither begotten nor does he proceed from another. His unique *auctoritas* (origination) accounts for this, not any diversity in the divine nature since there is none. The Son is fittingly sent by the Father because the Father eternally begets him. No inequality results from either this begetting or sending. (*On the Trinity,* 4,20,28f) The mission of the Son differs from that of the Holy Spirit in that the latter does not assume a human nature in the unity of a person. Christ comes into the world (Jn 1,10f) where he had been as God, but where he had not been as God's Wisdom manifest. Just as Christ appears in creaturely form, so the Spirit is "shown forth visibly in the appearances of a creature in time." (2,5,10) This we call the mission of the Holy Spirit, even though there is no question of his assuming a creature such as the dove or tongues of flame in the way the Word assumed a human nature in the body of the virgin Mary. The "form of a servant" adhered to the unity of a person whereas those other appearances (dove, fire) were visible at need and immediately fell away.

Augustine asks whether the theophanies experienced by our fathers under the former covenant were manifestations of the Father, the Son, or the Spirit, or of all without distinction. He answers that the three persons are equally invisible, hence no theophany can be a true appearance of any one of them. The manifestations therefore were a means used by the entire godhead to convey truth to the patriarchs, and this they did through the ministry of creatures. These creatures were angels, even though we cannot understand how they could have acted in what Augustine takes to be a prefiguring of the incarnation. He says he has no doubt that this is what took place. The angelic activity was not a true incarnation. Yet how exactly it was done he cannot say. (3,11,26; 6,21,31)

"But when your Advocate has come, whom I will send
you from the Father—the Spirit of truth that issues
from the Father—he will bear witness to me." (Jn 15,
26) (*Last Supper,* by an anonymous thirteenth-century
Italian painter; Isaac Delgado Museum of Art, New
Orleans; courtesy Samuel H. Kress Collection)

CHAPTER FOUR

FROM AUGUSTINE
TO THE COUNCILS
OF REUNION

St. Augustine logically follows the Cappadocians in any history of trinitarian thought. We should be untrue to the actual development of this dogma, however, if we omitted tracing carefully the course of trinitarian piety during the anti-Arian reaction. The Arians had used the ancient Catholic prayers and doxologies addressed to God the Father *through* the Son (or *through* Christ) *in* the Holy Spirit to support their contention that the latter two persons were not truly God. At Antioch in 350 the above form of the doxology (i.e., "Glory be to the Father, etc. . . .") yielded to a traditional Syrian form based on Mt 28,19, "*and* to the Son, *and* to the Holy Spirit," as part of the Nicaean response to the Arian denial. Feelings on the question became so intense that the patriarch of Antioch, Flavian, required that the prayer be recited inaudibly. A treatise by St. Basil *On the Holy Spirit* in 375 justified the Catholic sense of the older formulation, but also defended a newer one (*metá . . . sýn*, i.e., along with), which stressed the equality of the persons. St. John Chrysostom used this form in his sermons from 390 onward. St. Basil in his doxologies takes pains to insist on the Son's divinity, inevitably somewhat to the derogation of his mediatory function.

TRINITARIAN PIETY, THE FRUIT OF ANTI-ARIANISM

Belief in the Trinity was stressed increasingly in the fifth century. Christ the Maker of all (*Panto-krátōr*) was much spoken of and represented, whereas Christ the Mediator receded from Christian consciousness. Teutonic tribes like the Visigoths as they became Christians tended to be Arians because emperors like Valens were committed to the heresy. Wulfila the Goth simply took over from Byzantium the Seleucia-Rimini creed of 359, which declared the Father to be like (*homoíos*) the Son. (Cf. p. 65 above.) J. A. Jungmann cites evidence in support of the thesis that whereas the Romans practiced the Catholic faith the Teutons, who ruled in northern Italy, southern France, Spain, and North Africa from the fifth century onward, practiced the Arian belief. (*Pastoral Liturgy*, pp. 16f.)

The end of more than a century of struggle came in 589 when the Visigoths of Spain became Catholics. The reconciliation process required a profession of faith in the formula, "Glory be to the Father through the Son in the Holy Spirit. (III Council of Toledo, *Can.* 19; *Mansi* 9,986) At the same time recitation of the Creed of Nicaea-Constantinople was specified in the West for the first time.

Despite this, the Arians continued to taunt the Catholics that the phrase *"per Christum* [or *Filium*] . . . *in Spiritu Sancto"* favored their subordinationist position. The Catholic response took the form of confessing the "one Trinity, inseparable God." (Jungmann, p. 25, citing

CSEL 7,34) When Arian Vandals in Spain forcibly baptized a Roman maiden and challenged her to divide the blessed Trinity she declared her belief that "the Father with the Son, and Holy Spirit, were of one substance and essence." The unity of the godhead and the equality in essence of the Father and the Son were the strong features of Catholic anti-Arian polemic. Catholics sacrificed to the Trinity, they said, even if the Father only is addressed.

When modalism erupted in Spain through the Priscillianist heresy, the same stress had to be given to the distinction of the persons as to the unity of the essence. The major emphasis of the sixth and seventh centuries was on prayer addressed indiscriminately to the Father, to Christ, and to the blessed Trinity. Prefaces of the Mass were tampered with in notable departures from the prayer patterns of the early Church. Thus the ancient call to sacrifice came to read, "Let us offer worthy thanks (eucharist) and praise to God and to our Lord Jesus Christ who is in heaven." Perhaps the concern of that age with the question of the coequal and undivided Trinity is best summed up in Canon 13 of the Synod of Toledo, referred to above: "Whosoever will not believe that the Son of God and the Holy Spirit must be glorified and praised along with the Father, let him be anathema." (*Mansi* 9,986)

Prayers addressed to Christ and to the Trinity were multiplied in this period. Sometimes it remained doubtful exactly to whom they were spoken (e.g., "O Lord. . . ."). In any case, the mediation of Christ was almost thoroughly submerged. *The net result of all this was that stress on the divine Trinity led paradoxically to a progressive de-emphasis of the role of the three persons in the work of saving mankind.* True faith in the Trinity—which was interpreted to mean the mysterious interrelation of the persons rather than the primitive good news of salvation in Jesus Christ—became the center of orthodox concern. People prayed that they might die persevering in trinitarian faith. What was new in all this, of course, was not concern with "threeness" in God, for that was as old as the New Testament itself and the earliest liturgies and creeds; the new element was the identification of the inner life of God with the core of Catholic faith rather than the mighty deed of God the Father to save man through his Son in the Holy Spirit.

By the seventh century in Ireland, the eighth in Gaul, and the ninth with respect to Western sacramentaries generally, the trinitarian Mass which takes its tone largely from the preface was fully formed. Boniface, Patrick, and the rest of the missionaries of Europe brought Catholic faith and piety of this trinitarian sort to the pagans. The exposition of the Sign of the Cross took over in medieval catechisms as the briefest compendium possible of the faith of the Church.

FROM BOETHIUS TO THE DIALECTICIANS

As to speculative concern during the post-Arian period, Augustine was unquestionably the great figure in trinitarian theology until the time of St. Thomas Aquinas. Aquinas in turn was prepared for by the activity of Abelard, Anselm, and Peter the Lombard. There were few significant theological developments immediately after the time of Augustine. His contribution, it will be recalled, had been stress upon the divine essence whence all God's activity outside himself (*ad extra*) proceeds. He described the generation of the Son as the act of thought of the Father, following Tertullian in his analysis of the terms Word and Wisdom. Augustine was inclined to see certain vestiges of the Trinity in nature, especially in the human spirit as it remembers, has an understanding of, and loves God.

Boethius, the Alexandrian-trained philosopher and statesman (d. 524), contributed the phrase "substance comprehends unity, relation multiplies trinity" to Western theology in his brief treatise *How the Trinity Is One God and Not Three.* (Ch. 6) This, coupled with a phrase from St. Gregory of Nazianz, would lead to the formulation of the famous dictum of Anselm, "All is unity except where the opposition of relation enters in." (*On the Procession of the Holy Spirit,* 7)

The sixth-century Alexandrian, John Philoponus (d. c. 565), attempted a reconciliation of Catholic faith with Aristotelian thought. His synthesis seemingly had as a by-product the error of tritheism. This stemmed from a failure to stress the unity of nature of the three divine persons. John's initial flaw was in not distinguishing adequately between nature and person. This thinker progressed from a verbal monophysite position (Severus of Antioch, his teacher, had said "out of two natures, the godhead and the manhood, one Emmanuel and one incarnate nature of the God-Logos emerges") to a profession of faith in three natures—or persons—who are brought together by a mere mental abstraction. He denied believing in three Gods, but the wording of II Constantinople (553) was against him. Incorporating the terminology of the Cappadocians, that fifth ecumenical council said:

1. If anyone does not acknowledge the one nature (*phýsin*) or substance (*ousían*) of the Father, Son, and Holy Spirit, their one virtue and power, a consubstantial Trinity, one godhead worshipped in three persons (*hypostásesin*) or characters (*prosōpois*), let him be anathema. For there is one God and Father from whom are all things, and one Lord Jesus Christ through whom are all things, and one Holy Spirit, in whom are all things. (D213[421])

ABELARD   A similar error recurs in the West in the career of Peter Abelard (d. 1142). This incurable dialectician held that the ancient pagan philosophers had at least vestigial ideas of the Trinity and the incarnation, and that faith that had not the support of reason was only an opinion, a supposition. He found himself maintaining in his treatise *On the Divine Unity and Trinity* (*Theologia Christiana*) that Power belonged to the Father alone, Wisdom to the Son alone, and Goodness to the Holy Ghost alone. Thus did the three complete each other and form one principle of operation. The Council of Soissons (1121) burned that treatise, while that of Sens condemned him in 1140, attributing to him such errors as that "the Father is full power, the Son a certain power, and the Holy Spirit no power" (D368[721]), "the Holy Spirit is not of the *substance* [omnipotence] of the Father [or of the Son]" (D369[722]), and "the Holy Spirit is the soul of the universe." (D370[722]) Abelard is generally dismissed as a modalist. His worst offense was probably an unsuccessful attempt to keep the divine unity intact by virtue of a thoroughly inadequate scheme of appropriation. The nominalism that was the curse of the twelfth-century logicians kept him from achieving the eminence as a theologian that he craved. Father, Son, and Holy Spirit are "three names," "three causes" for him. Divine Power and Wisdom instil fear, but Goodness (*Benignitas*) begets love. He is forever expressing the mystery in full Catholic language, then being led away by the *vocabulum* or *nomen* of a particular divine person to speak of him as one of three manifestations of the single substance.

After his final condemnation by the Council of Sens, which he could not stave off, Abelard drew up a beautiful testimony of Catholic faith in the form of a letter to his onetime paramour, Heloïse, from whom he had long been separated. In it he expressed belief in the Son's equality with the Father in eternity, in power, in will, in operation. He reprobated the error of Sabellius by name and confessed the Holy Spirit equal and consubstantial in all things with the Father and the Son—though he could

85

not resist calling him "the Goodness" as he had so often done in his writings. (*Letter* 17)

ROSCELIN   Roscelinus of Compiègne was an early figure in nominalistic thought, the school that denied the reality of universal ideas. The latter were held to be only words or names, hence without objective value. Applying this tenet to trinitarian teaching, he arrived at the notion of three different substances for the divine persons, united only in their equality of will and power. It was in reaction to the supposed "tritheism" of Roscelinus that St. Anselm first entered the trinitarian lists.

The difficulties encountered by logic with this mystery derived from the supposition that the godhead was subject to analysis like any being. The assumption was more absurd than arrogant, but it led to no fewer errors for that reason. Basic to the problem of terminology was Boethius' definition of person which was still in undisputed possession: "an individual substance rational by nature." Rufinus of Aquileia (d. 410), who translated much of Origen's work from Greek into Latin, had rendered the word *hypóstasis* into *subsistentia* rather than *substantia* so as to keep it a denomination of person rather than of nature in trinitarian use. The I Lateran Council of 649 against the monothelites used "subsistence" in that sense, namely a concrete, existent individual who in the case of divinity is the possessor of the divine substance in common with two other persons: "one God in three consubstantial subsistences of equal glory." (D254[501]) The temptation of the nominalists was to apply Boethius' definition of person to the divine persons without qualification. Finding themselves with three substances—"substance" not in the pre-fifth century sense of *hypóstasis* or person but divine essences—they then had recourse to a "single divine substance [supra-]rational by nature" which was distinguished as to persons only in a logical, not a real way. *They reduced the three persons in God to modes of his being, in other words, while holding fast for the most part to the ancient creedal language.* When their ambivalent stand was discovered, as Abelard's was by his foe St. Bernard, they were condemned as heretics.

ANSELM   St. Anselm of Bec, who died in 1109 as archbishop of Canterbury, framed the Boethian difficulty by saying: "In the supreme Being, just as there are not more substances than one, so there are not more persons than one." (*Monologium,* 78) Individual substances are ordinarily subject to accidents, though this is not the case with the divine substance. The word substance is usually applied to individual beings which subsist in plurality—but again, this is not true of the three divine persons who are not three beings. Anselm's final formulation despairs of applying terms univocally, that is, in the same sense, to God and creatures: "The supreme Being, which is subject to no accidents, cannot properly be called a substance, except as the word *substance* is used in the same sense with the word *Essence*. Hence, on this ground, namely of necessity, that supreme and one Trinity or trinal unity may justly be called one Essence and three Persons or three Substances." (*Ibid.*) Aquinas, following Aristotle, would hold that Anselm could only have meant by his final phrase "*first* substances," that is, individual subsistents rational by nature. Such, he says, was Boethius' understanding of person. The term "second substance" therefore is available as the equivalent of nature or essence. (*S.Th.*, 1,29, 1 ad 2)

RICHARD OF ST. VICTOR   It will remain for Richard of St. Victor (d. 1173) to deliver the question from the impasse Boethius brought it to—namely that the Trinity is an individual substance but not a person— by defining a divine person as an "incommunicable existence of divine nature." (*On the Trinity*, 4,22) Richard, like his teacher Hugh of St. Victor, was interested in framing convincing theological arguments— *rationes necessariae*, as he called them. He differed from Abelard and Gilbert de la Porrée (bishop of Poitiers, d. 1154) in that he recognized theology's full dependence on faith whereas they tended to think dialectical technique adequate to exploring realities in the realm of divinity. Their reliance on the predicates and categories of logic seems naïve to us at this distance. Anyone who caught them at their game could hold them up to censure as rationalists, as indeed St. Bernard of Clairvaux did. But in those years to press the legitimate claims of theology as rooted in revelation was to run the risk of seeming to mistrust reason.

Thus, when Gilbert in applying his metaphysical principles to the godhead taught that although God was entirely "simple" the three persons were one God only by reason of the "form" of divinity common to all, Bernard pounced on him severely. Gilbert had said by way of analogy with humanity, which constitutes men as individuals, that the divine essence constitutes the members of the Trinity divine persons but is not itself God. "There is one essence *by which* they are divine but *which* is not divine." Bernard's response is classic: "Let it be written with iron upon adamant, let it be carved upon flint, that the divine essence, form, 87 nature, goodness, wisdom, virtue, and power are each truly God." Although quite correct in his affirmation, Bernard by the force of his rhetoric and his antidialectic spirit seems to resist the attempt to put intellectual inquiry in the service of theology. It should be noted that he failed to obtain a condemnation of Gilbert's trinitarian teaching at the Council of Rheims in 1148. (D 389ff[745])

PETER THE LOMBARD

Abelard had written in his *Introduction to Theology,* Book 2: "Now therefore it remains for us, after having laid down the foundation of authority, to place upon it the buttress of reasoning." The best-known medieval theologian to achieve the needed juncture between buttress and foundation—represented by Abelard (*ratio*) and Hugh of St. Victor (*auctoritas, traditio*)—was Peter the Lombard, who died in 1160 as archbishop of Paris after only one year in that office. The first of the Lombard's four books of *Sententiae* dealt with God. He stressed positive theology, that is, the sources of belief in the mystery of the Trinity. Only after that initial stress did he apply the categories of dialectic. It is to be recalled that the chief complaint of monastic theologians like Bernard against the scholastics was that the latter since the ninth century had been applying the method of questioning or disputing to divine things, whereas they, the monks, confined this technique to the liberal arts. Just as in the fourth century, so in the twelfth, the charge was made that the "new men" employed philosophical terms rather than biblical to describe the divine mysteries. (The interesting paradox of the present period cannot escape us.) To this was added the accusation of mere curiosity about the mysteries. "This sacrament is great," wrote Bernard, "it must be venerated, not scrutinized." (*On Contemplation,* 5,18)

Peter the Lombard was not free of the suspicion of rationalism, but when his trinitarian teaching received approbation at the IV Lateran Council (1215) against the Cistercian abbot Joachim of Flora (d. 1202) he acquired the beginnings of the respectability that would give him absolute theological pre-eminence until the seventeenth century. Joachim ascribed to the Lombard belief in a fourfold unity of God, namely belief in the three persons and in addition the divine essence which is common to them. The council cleared Peter of the charge and condemned Joachim as a heretic.

> We believe and confess with Peter the Lombard that there is one su-
> preme reality—incomprehensible, ineffable—which is in truth Father,
> Son, and Holy Spirit; three persons, both simultaneously and taken
> singly: therefore in God there is trinity only, not quaternity; for what
> is proper to the three persons is that reality (*res*) which is substance,
> essence, or divine nature. This alone is the principle of all else; no
> other can be found. This reality neither begets nor is begotten nor
> proceeds; it is the Father who begets, the Son who is begotten, and
> the Holy Spirit who proceeds; wherefore the distinctions are in the
> persons and the unity is in the nature." (D432[804])

Before returning to the Lombard we should not omit mentioning
Joachim's theory, found in his writings compiled as *The Eternal Gospel*,
of successive ages of the world under the dominance of the Father (the
Old Testament), the Son (the New Testament), and the Holy Ghost
(the Church up to 1260)! After the latter date—which he arrived at by
means of the genealogies in St. Matthew's prologue—there would come
the age of the Trinity, which was to be "the rule of the monks" in a spirit
of poverty. Freedom from war, the conversion of the Jews, and reunion
with the Greeks would be some of the benefits of this final age. Joachim
contrasted it as Johannine with the Petrine Church of the period up until
then. His apocalyptic view provided the vocabulary for the later construc-
tions of Hegel and Schelling, popularized in the symbolic conception,
"the third Reich."

Peter the Lombard attempted a synthesis of patristic teaching but
his use of Augustine outstripped that of any other Father. He quoted
the bishop of Hippo more than a thousand times (more than 90 per cent
of his total quotations), while Hilary and Ambrose are cited only between
thirty and forty times each. Chrysostom occurs about twenty times, Origen
a dozen, and the Cappadocians even less than that. His conservation of
Augustinian doctrine has caused his work to be referred to as "The Sentences [Opinions] of St. Augustine." The Lombard was heavy-handed
in comparison with Augustine's quick genius. When confronted with in-
consistencies in his own position, or among the Fathers generally, he
attempted a reconciliation. The chief trinitarian concern of Augustine
and the "Master of the Sentences" after him was the procession of the
divine persons. We shall trace its development immediately in St. Thomas
Aquinas (d. 1274), the prince of commentators on the four books of the
Lombard.

ST. THOMAS AQUINAS

Processions within the godhead, said Aquinas, are something we know about from Scripture. (Jn 8,42; 15,26) He defined a procession as a passage from origin to term. Within the godhead there is no cause and effect as in ordinary "exterior" activity; here, both origin and term are God. The interior or immanent character of human mental processes, however, make them suitable if pale images of eternal activity within the godhead. "Divine procession must be understood as an intellectual emanation, somewhat in the way the intellectual *verbum* proceeds from the intellect while remaining there." (*S.Th.*, 1ª,27,1) Aquinas then takes the scriptural term Word and the revealed fact that the Son is begotten and synthesizes them in the notion that *the Word proceeds from the Father by way of perfect, that is intellectual, generation.* All the elements of generation are present: the activity of a living being, the principle (begetter) united to term (offspring), the likeness of offspring to begetter, and a unity in nature. "Therefore in God the procession of the Word is called a generation, and the Word which proceeds is known as Son." (*Ibid.*, a.2)

As to the procession of the Spirit, he comes "from the Father *and the Son*," in the phrase of the sixth-century Spanish addition to the creed of Nicaea-Constantinople. Aquinas says that "procession" is commonly used as a proper term for origin of any kind (*S.Th.*, 1ª,36,2), a true enough statement if one searches out its usage in the Septuagint translation of the Old Testament. The Eastern Fathers insist that *ekporeúesthai*, "proceed," is used by the New Testament writers to describe the Holy Spirit's relation to the Father only (Jn 15,26), and they use nonscriptural verbs like *proiénai* and *procheîsthai* for the relation of the Holy Spirit to the Son. St. Thomas sets this aside, being a man of the West who knows neither the New Testament in Greek nor the Oriental Fathers, by simply following the Vulgate's use of *procedere* for both the *ekporeúetai* of John 15,26 and the *exēlthon* of John 8,42. Jesus is invariably described as "coming forth" (*exerchésthai*) from his Father, a verb rendered by *"processi"* in John 8,42, but normally by *exire* (e.g., Jn 13,3; 16,27.28.30; 17,8). The gospels do not seem to distinguish procession from mission.

Aquinas' argument is undisturbed because he uses the vocabulary of human psychology rather than local movement. If the word "Word" directs us toward a procession by way of conception or thought, he holds, we are left with the other faculty of the soul, the will, whose tendency is to love. In a procession of love, "the beloved is in the lover, even as in the conception of a word the thing thought or said is in the thinker. Wherefore, we must conclude that besides the procession of the Word there is in God another procession which is a procession of Love." (*S.Th.*, 1ª,27,3) Since the divine processions must be immanent acts in God, and since such acts can be but two in an intelligent and divine nature—namely to know a thought and to will it—in God there can be but two processions, those of the Word and of Love. (Cf. *ibid.*, a.5.)

The twentieth-century theologian de Régnon remarks the almost geometric progress of this argument of Thomas, derived from Augustine by way of Anselm. (*Études . . . sur la Sainte Trinité*, 2,143f.) It is all but identified with the trinitarian dogma itself in the minds of most Catholics of the West. Unfortunately for its status as the faith of the universal Church, as the Melchite Patriarch of Egypt Monsignor Zoghby remarked at the First Session of the II Vatican Council, it is a development largely unknown to the East, at least in this form. St. Thomas' insistence on the analogous character of his argument exonerates him from the charge that he has made God in the image of man. (*S.Th.*, 1ª,32,1 and ad 2) In question 32 he is at pains to establish that a Trinity of divine persons cannot be proved from reason; the fact that intellect is not univocal in God and us is of course the basic reason why the analogy breaks down. Aquinas was therefore not in the least confused by the analogous character of his exposition. The question is, are other Western Christians equally clear? Even the concepts "intellect and will" as human faculties or powers of soul leave very few modern psychologists at ease, conjuring up in them visions of split-level man.

In any case the procession of the Holy Spirit by way of love has never been made the subject of dogmatic definition by the Church. The New Testament affirms that there are goings forth (processions) in God. The principle of reason that in God the word "procession" must be interpreted as spiritually as possible is then applied. From this, four affirmations result by way of deduction: in an intelligent nature the first procession is by way of thought; in God, thought fulfills all the requirements for true generation; the second procession in God is by way of will; in God there are but two processions, one by way of word or utterance and the other by way of will.

St. Thomas had earlier argued (in his *Commentary on the Sentences*

[I,2,1,4]) that God is supremely good and loves perfectly, but that since he cannot give himself perfectly to creatures, nor are they attractive enough to be loved above all, he satisfies the requirement of perfect self-giving in the divine begetting and then loves perfectly a perfect beloved who is distinct from him but of the one nature. Later he would write that the manner whereby God is in himself as known in knower is described by the terms *generation, father, son, word,* all of which imply a specific likeness. But the manner whereby God is in himself as beloved in lover is described by the term *breath* or *spirit.* (Cf. *Compendium of Theology,* 46.)

"The love which loves the supreme good which is God is so excellent it is called *holy.* . . . Fittingly, therefore, we speak of the Spirit which is God's love of himself as the Holy Spirit." (*Ibid.,* 47) Following Augustine, Thomas describes the relations in God as subsistent in the divine substance, not accidental.(48) Although God's being and understanding and loving are identical with himself (8 *On Power,* 1), when he understands himself a Word is conceived, and when he loves himself the Holy Spirit—who is "of the love whereby God is in himself as the beloved in the lover"—proceeds from the Father and the Son. (*Compendium of Theology,* 49)

St. Thomas in using the human situation as his analogue for the divine says that "the presence of the beloved in the lover comes first from the principle of love and next from the beloved being held in mind, that is, from the word of the beloved which is conceived." (*Ibid.*) In other words, the Father is the principle who first has an idea of himself (Son) and then loves what he knows, the beloved (Spirit) being in the lover (Father) by way of word or concept (Son) and therefore coming forth from both. It is an essential note of Thomas's trinitarian doctrine, of course, that the processions or emanations in God terminate within the divine being. The generation of the Son is by way of a reflection on the self, the procession of the Spirit by way of an impulsion or motion toward the self. (*S.Th.,* 1ª,27,4)

In God the persons exist as really, not logically, distinct relations. Anything numerical about the Three is by way of analogy with quantity in creatures. (*S.Th.,* 1,30,1, ad 4 and 3) The divine relations arise from an activity immanent in God which connotes nothing of before and after, active and passive, perfect and imperfect. The real and mutual relation between the Word and its Begetter is rooted in the identity of God's mind and its activity: the two are co-essential to each other; no cleavage in unity of essence is implied. (*10 On Power,* 1)

The concept of relation occurred first in trinitarian theology in the controversy of the Greek Fathers against the Eunomians (Macedonians). A relation is the order in which one thing or person stands to another. In God, relations are the necessary implication of the processions. The vocabulary of relation includes principle or subject (e.g., Father), foundation (e.g., fatherhood), and term (e.g., Son). In creatures there is accidental modification, hence a "being in" (*esse in*) a certain state, for example, a man and his corpulence, a coin and its roundness. God is free of accident, hence each of the Three is marked by the pure relation (*respectus purus*) of persons who "are to" each other (*esse ad*), and by an *esse in* which is substantial (i.e., nonaccidental). The latter consists in the divine essence which all have perfectly and without distinction. Opposition among the Three arises from *being to* (*the others*) only. This relation of opposition is sufficient to explain the persons. Nothing else will satisfactorily do so, since all are formally constituted in their perfection by the same thing, namely the divine essence.

"Fatherhood," therefore, is a real and incommunicable relation which the Father has to the Son. It signifies a *being to* (*another*). "Father," on the other hand, since it is the name of someone identical with the divine essence, signifies a *being in and to*. The relations are distinct from the divine essence by a virtual major distinction, as it is called (or logical distinction with a foundation in reality); this is the *being* of persons *in* essence. The distinction is real when they *are* (something) *to* each other in the mutual opposition of persons.

The only things in God that are really distinct are the opposed relations which are of origin. (Cf. *S.Th.,* 1ª,29,4.) It is by these that the persons are constituted. The persons are distinct because they are incommunicable. Their *being in* the divine nature comprises their reality, their *being to* each other as principle and term, their relation. Real or subsistent relation therefore constitutes the persons. The Father communicates everything to the Son except his Fatherhood, which is incommunicable. Father and Son (Father *through* Son, the Greeks would say) communicate everything to the Spirit except their Fatherhood and Sonship which are incommunicable.

All these matters Aquinas discusses in the *Summa Theologiae* 1ª,28,3 and 4. He has dealt elsewhere with what he considers the im-   *93* plication of Gilbert de la Porrée that the divine relations are only logical and not real, hence the persons not really mutually distinct. (8 *On Power,* 2) He observes that the relations of Fatherhood and Sonship are not matched by a proper term to describe what comes forth by love—an uncatalogued activity—and to describe the resulting relations. The relation of the principle is called a breathing or *spiration,* and the answering relation is called a proceeding forth or *procession*—although both terms denote origin rather than relation. (Cf. *S.Th.,* 1ª,28,4.)

Fatherhood in its perfection describes the relation of divine person to divine person; thence it is used in a derived sense to include God's relationship to creatures. (1ª,33,3) In knowing himself God knows all creatures. St. Thomas would be more at ease with the idea that the entire deity is Father to humanity than that the eternal Father is, in a special (i.e., nonappropriated) way.

The unique Word is expressive of God the Father and all creation. (1ª,33,3) The truth of things is greater in the Word than it is in created reality, though names are more accurately applied to persons and things as real subjects existing in their nature than to their existence in the Word. (4 *On Truth,* 6)

Loving and holding dear are essential to the divine nature, but when *love* means the Love that arises in the deity and *holding dear* means a breathing forth of affection, then *Love* is the name of a person and *holding dear* manifests a personal activity and is a personal term, like *uttering* the Word or *begetting* the Son. (*S.Th.,* 1ª,37,1) The reason for any gift is love. Love is the first gift. The Holy Ghost comes forth as the substance of love, and *Gift* is his proper name. (1ª,38,2)

The subsistent relations in God are three, being the three persons who *are to* each other. It is commonly said that the relations in God are four: Fatherhood, Sonship, active Spiration, and passive Spiration. The first two have a perfect mutuality. The third is the single deed of the Father and Son in producing the Spirit, whereas the fourth is the Spirit as he comes forth. The third is not a really distinct relation, only a means to describe the single principle whence he proceeds. This principle is no different from the person already constituted Father by begetting the Son, in the theory of the Greeks, and is Father and Son together *as a single principle* in the theory of the West.

Why does not the Father have a second Son in the Holy Spirit? "Because the latter does not come forth from him by begetting," is the best answer St. Thomas can provide. He proceeds, rather, by love or gift.

94

The two who are responsible for the Spirit's person are already constituted persons as they do so, hence his being breathed forth by them does nothing to their subsistent relationship. How a second can proceed from the Father after the first, but not a third or fourth, is an absolute mystery.

THE QUESTION OF THE *FILIOQUE*

The position of the Son with respect to the Father in the Spirit's proceeding from the Father is so controverted that it has frequently been isolated as *the* great point of difference between East and West. The Council of Florence (1438–45) long afterward reported the form the difference took by saying that "according to the Greek Fathers the Son is indeed also the cause [*aítion*], but according to the Latin Fathers, the principle [*principium*] of the subsistence of the Holy Spirit." (D 691[1300]) In saying this it was simply repeating the "reunion formula" of the Council of Lyons of 1274. (D 460[850]) From the beginning of Western writing the Spirit was taught as proceeding from the Father *and* the Son, for example by Tertullian (*Against Praxeas*, 8), Novatian (*On the Trinity*, 16), Ambrose (*On the Holy Spirit*, 1,15,172), and Hilary. (*On the Trinity*, 2,29) In the East the Spirit generally proceeds from the Father *by* or *through* (*dià*) the Son, though the phrase *and from* the Son also has an Oriental history.

As to the former, the mode of procession, Origen says that as all things come from the Father through the Son, the Spirit is the "most worthy and first" of such beings. (*On John*, 2,6) The Holy Spirit is brought forth from (*hypò*) the Father through (*dià*) Christ. For Athanasius, the Son has a similar relation to the Father as the Holy Spirit has to the Son. The Spirit is in God by the Word; his sanctifying and enlightening power is said to proceed from the Father, since the Son who proceeds from the Father makes it shine, sends, and gives it. (Cf. *To Serapion*, 3,1,5,6; 1,20.) Similarly in Cyril of Jerusalem, Basil, and Gregory of Nyssa descriptions of the mystery name the Holy Spirit as the Spirit of Christ, *through whom* he comes in turn (*metadídōsin*) from the Father. All confess that the Spirit is in some way from the Son, although the Father is the main principle of fecundity. Epiphanius is almost alone by the year 400 in saying of the Holy Spirit, "He is between [*en mésōi*] the Father and the Son, he is from the Father and the Son. (*The Firmly Anchored Man*, 8) Another formula of the same writer is "pro-

95

ceeding from the Father, receiving from the Son." (*Ibid.*, 119; cf. D 13[44])

Efforts have been made—successfully, it would seem—to trace the procession formula "and from the Son" to Alexandria. (Cf. de Régnon, *op. cit.*, 3e série,2,91ff.) The claim is made that Ambrose copied it from Didymus and that Hilary got it from his sojourn in the East. This may be, but it was never the dominant tradition in the East where the processions were always thought of in a straight line. In fact the formula first came through clearly in an anti-Arian creed of a fifth-century synod at Toledo (*Can*. 445); its use followed in numerous other Spanish synods (e.g., III Toledo, 589) and culminated in that of Braga. (675) From there the phrase was taken up by synods at Gentilly in Gaul (787) and Frankfort (794), and copied by the service books of Charlemagne. Theologians at Charlemagne's court accused the Greeks of omitting this phrase when the Emperor could not get acknowledgment of his claims from Byzantium. Pope Leo III wrote to Charlemagne that although he himself believed that the Spirit did proceed from the Son, it was wrong to tamper with the wording of the creed.

In 867 Photius, patriarch of Constantinople, wrote an encyclical letter to the other patriarchs of the East accusing Rome of heresy for allowing Germanic missionaries in Bulgaria to use the *filioque*. At a council summoned by that letter, Pope Nicholas I was deposed and excommunicated. The IV Council of Constantinople (869–70) condemned and anathematized Photius (D341[661f]), who subsequently was restored (877) and died after nine years spent in full communion with the Roman bishops John VIII through Stephen V.

In 1009 Pope Sergius IV sent a copy of the interpolated creed to Patriarch Sergius of Constantinople, and for his heresy was left off the diptychs of that church (lists for commemoration in the liturgy). This act was tantamount to a declaration of a rupture of intercommunion. Five years later at the coronation of Henry II the papacy finally adopted the *filioque* in practice. In 1054, when the legates of Pope Leo IX excommunicated the patriarch of Constantinople Michael Cerularius, omission of the *filioque* was given as one of the reasons.

The theological differences—apart from the question of an addition to a conciliar creed without conciliar authorization—are summed up in the claims of the East that by the *filioque* the Father is derogated from as the sole principle (*archē*) in the godhead, and that the West has deserted scriptural usage in confusing the Spirit's temporal mission, that

96

is, his being sent by the Son in time, with his eternal procession from the Father. (Cf. p. 90 above.) If the West says—as it did at the "reunion councils" of Lyons and Florence—that the Spirit proceeds from Father and Son "as from a single principle," then, says the East, it not only fails to escape the charge of ditheism (two sources of origin in God) but is to be accused of confusing and commingling two divine persons. All in all, the Eastern concept of a *monarchía* of the Father who begets and breathes forth Two who are distinct from him is not readily reconciled with the Western idea of a single divine essence distinguished as to persons by activity interior to the godhead. The ancient difference of stress on persons and essence keeps recurring in every age.

Many have held that the East and the West do not differ on the substance of trinitarian faith but only on its wording, since "and from the Son" does not differ necessarily from "through the Son." If the Father begets the Son as his eternal "first act," there is a sense in which all else he does, including breathing forth the Spirit eternally, is done through the Son. The explanatory phrase "as from a single principle," in this supposition, is open to an interpretation in harmony with the writings of the Eastern Fathers. Eastern insistence that the Spirit proceeds from the Father *alone* relies on the silence of John 15,26, coupled with a disregard for the East's own lively tradition on the proceeding of the Spirit from the Father through the Son. The West, similarly, needs to be careful that it does not confuse a theological development with the ancient faith, on the false principle that development as such is right. It should be recalled, after all, that no Eastern Catholic is required to say the *filioque*. Many prefer to do so as symbolic of their communion with Rome, but in the Byzantine-rite churches in the city of Rome this phrase is not heard!

At the extended debates in the opening sessions of Florence, held in Ferrara in the autumn of 1438, the East clung to the position that the introduction of the *filioque* was "another faith" in the sense reprobated by Ephesus. That fifth-century council had declared that no other faith than its own could be introduced in the Church. Andrew of Rhodes and Cesarini responded for the Latins (against Mark Eugenicus and Bessarion for the East) that the phrase was a legitimate development in faith, not an addition: something roughly comparable to the creedal additions of I Constantinople to Nicaea. The West's case was that the phrase "from the Father" implicitly contains "and from the Son," since "All that the Father has is mine, and that is why I said, 'Everything that he [the Spirit]

97

makes known to you he draws from what is mine.'" (Jn 16,15) We should conclude by observing that the East preferred above all else at Florence not to argue the case theologically but to stress the illegitimacy of an addition to the creed by a part of the Church rather than by the whole Church.

THE RELATION OF MISSION TO PROCESSION

These enervating debates have been considered by both East and West a matter of fidelity to Christ and orthodox faith, though in fact they seem like a struggle between parties who consider that what is legitimate development among them is innovation when it comes from the other camp. One thing that is clear is that the biblical data on eternal processions never appear in a "pure state." They are so closely identified with the sending to earth of the Word (in the incarnation) or the Spirit (in the Church) that to fasten on one New Testament verb and say, "This means eternal procession only," and on another, "This clearly connotes temporal mission only," is to miss the dynamism of New Testament speech.

In fact, nothing is revealed to us exclusively in terms of eternal act in God. All is told in terms of his deed to save us. St. Thomas distinguishes clearly between coming forth and being sent, as regards divine persons. (S.Th., 1ª,43,1) The former has to do with the eternal origins of Son and Spirit, the latter with their manifestations in time. Divine processions need no object such as the humanity of Jesus in the incarnation or the Church through the souls of the just in the sending of the Holy Spirit. Nonetheless St. Thomas calls the eternal begetting of the Son "the exemplar of all making" and the Father's love for the Son (this theologian's explanation of the origin of the Spirit) "the exemplar of all granting of love to creatures." (I Sent., 14,1,1) This legitimate enough theological thought takes its stance with God in eternity. To say that the saving deeds of God in time are patterned on the eternal life and love within him is surely correct. In fact, however, we learned that the Son had come from his Father to earth, and that returning to his Father he would send his Spirit from the Father to his friends on earth who had received him, before we knew anything of their eternal mutual relations. *It is from these data of human history that we discover that things are somehow similar in the Godhead.* Our terms of reference for the inner

98

trinitarian life are *not* the spiritual processes of the creature man, therefore, but the drama of salvation. God is, within himself, somewhat as he
is in his dealings with us. Our chief clue to the mystery of the Trinity
is the mystery of our redemption. But the redemption is not only a thing
of the past; it is a reality of the present. St. Thomas shows his awareness
of this when he says, "A divine person is *sent* [the Son] when he comes
to a creature in a new way, and *given* [the Spirit] when possessed by a
creature. Neither situation comes about except through sanctifying
grace." (*S.Th.*, 1ª,43,3)

This is simply to say what the Greek Fathers were fond of arguing,
that the best testimony to the reality of the three persons in one God is
the Christian in grace. Such a one bears their stamp. They dwell in him.
Whoever knows him knows them.

"Here is the proof that we dwell in him and he dwells in us: he has imparted his Spirit to us . . . and if a man acknowledges that Jesus is the Son of God, God dwells in him and he dwells in God." (1 Jn 4, 14.16) (Drawing by Fritz Eichenberg; courtesy Catholic Art Education, Blauvelt, N.Y.)

CHAPTER FIVE

THE INDWELLING
OF THE
DIVINE THREE

We proceed from the fact of the Christian in grace to our final consideration, namely how the Three are at work to sanctify us men. The scholastic tradition has it that, since the divine persons are inseparable in nature, whatever they achieve outside the godhead is fundamentally an action of this divine nature. The metaphysical principle employed is that all actions of the Trinity which are directed toward a result outside the inner life of God (*operationes ad extra*) are common to all three persons. Although the New Testament and the Fathers of the Church traditionally appropriate the work of sanctification to the Holy Spirit, it is said, it must in fact be the work of all Three acting as one. It might be mentioned parenthetically that the necessary and direct involvement of the Three when attribution is made to a particular person (e.g., creation to the Father, redemption to the Son), is the result of their mutual coinherence. This existence of the divine persons *in* each other testified to in the gospel of St. John (1,18; 10,38; 14,9.11) is known to the Greek Fathers as *perichōrēsis* ("compenetration," lit. a "dancing about"). In sixteenth-century Latin translation this becomes either *circumincessio,* which is like the Greek in stressing the dynamic aspect, or *circuminsessio* which has them "seated within" each other rather than in motion. The Council of Florence expressed this truth by saying, "The Father is wholly (*totus*) in the Son, wholly in the Holy Spirit; the Son wholly in the Father, wholly in the Holy Spirit; the Holy Spirit wholly in the Father, wholly in the Son." (D704[1331])

Returning to the joint action of the Trinity through the divine nature in all external activity, we observe that not even the incarnation is exempt from this principle. There the human nature of Christ is in a unique relation to the Son—exactly how is incomprehensible to us—but the action of God bringing about this situation is an action of all Three. What this has meant practically to the West is that grace in man has been viewed as a work of efficient causality of the divine Trinity. God sanctifies men *as God,* that is, through his godhead or nature. A special relation of the Christian to any of the Three taken singly is therefore de-emphasized; all is a matter of appropriation. The Trinity becomes present to the soul through knowledge and love, the human activities that effect in man a special likeness to God. This presence of God to the creature is new and vital, and surpasses his presence to him as Creator.

Once more we see the practical results of the Western stress upon unity of nature. A lively trinitarian consciousness and piety has not developed since everything is achieved in us by an undifferentiated "God," if we may so speak.

Beginning with M. J. Scheeben in the middle of the last century and continuing with the writings of Th. de Régnon and E. Mersch, there has been a new insistence on the work of the individual Three in divinizing the Christian. The scholastic position, these theologians said, does not sufficiently attend to the language of Scripture and the

Fathers which normally attributes sanctification to the Spirit and in general assumes a more intimate relation with individual persons in God as they sanctify us. This type of thinking does not repudiate the scholastic teaching on grace. It declares it true and says it does not go far enough.

The pioneer in this effort was the seventeenth-century French theologian Dionysius Petavius (Petau) who held in his *Dogmata Theologica* that the relation of the Holy Spirit to the Christian in grace was not unlike that of the Word and his humanity. (John Calvin, incidentally, has what may almost be called an "incarnation of the Holy Spirit" as his basic principle of ecclesiology.) Petavius marshaled numerous texts, especially from St. Cyril of Alexandria, to the effect that the Holy Spirit is in us substantially (as he understood *ousidōs;* "personally" is probably a better translation) and not merely efficiently. By the communication of his person he makes us holy. There is in our sanctification something which is proper to the Holy Spirit and belongs to him alone. Even as the Word is in Christ as form to make this man God, so the Holy Spirit is in us to divinize us. The Father and the Holy Spirit are in Christ, not the Word only; similarly, all Three are in us in grace, but the Spirit in a unique way. Petavius very clearly avoided any intimation of a hypostatic union of the Holy Spirit with the Christian. He merely declared our union with him to be an absolutely unique case of moral (i.e., accidental) union.

Petavius was subject to much criticism for his departure from normal theological thinking. Scheeben denied anything proper to the Holy Spirit in divine activity *ad extra,* but he did ascribe a great pedagogical virtue to our use of the scheme of appropriations. The Trinity reveals itself to us in two ways, he said: by *prolongation,* of which the hypostatic union of the Word is the sole case, and by *imitation,* either in creation (natural order) or in grace (supernatural order). It is only when the divine nature is communicated to man that we have some idea of what generation in God is. The eternal Sonship is the exemplary cause of our adoptive sonship, giving it meaning and possibility. The "love and gift" of Father and Son, which the Spirit is necessarily, serves as the basis of the loving manner in which divine sonship is gratuitously given to us.

The specific difference in Scheeben's thought is his view that the common activity of the Three in the divine essence has as its effect that the persons sent to man and dwelling in him do so distinctly. The Father *comes* and the Son and Spirit are *sent* to the Christian. Actively taken, the indwelling of the Three is seen as an "impression," that is, a sign or seal. Passively their presence is the "possession" of the Christian soul. The Son comes as Image of the Father—which he is—the Spirit as Gift given for our enjoyment. God's Image is known by us; his Pledge or Gift is enjoyed by us. The Three possess the divine nature fully, each in a special way. Is it not the case, Scheeben asks, that each of the Three possesses the created nature of a Christian in a special way? For him the Spirit is the link with humanity, being the "outer limit" of the godhead, so to say. He is fittingly donated to man so that he can bring man into union with the other Two from whom he is never separated. He gives man the "sanctity of consecration"; he is the Spirit of the Son, and when he comes into hearts he gives them the possibility of sonship along with the only Son.

De Régnon follows Petavius except where the latter limits the formal work of our sanctification to the Holy Spirit. Instead he has each of the Three dwelling formally in the souls of the just by way of his proper subsistence. "In the supernatural order each divine person personally intervenes by means of a role which is proper to him and characteristic of him. . . . . Wherever the personal role of one divine person is manifested, we must affirm that the other two persons also intervene personally." (*Etudes de théologie positive sur la Sainte Trinité*, 4,536 and 537) De Régnon concludes to an "influence," distinct and proper to each person, of the members of the Trinity in the divinization of the Christian. Each of the Three comes with his own special and personal character: the Father as begetter, the Son as begotten, the Holy Spirit as the gift of the Two. Our sanctification is an effect common to all three persons, but each person keeps his own role.

Mersch's interesting theory posits incorporation into Christ as the link between the Christian and the divine Trinity. The relationship of mystical identity with Christ that comes at baptism brings in its train a relation of sonship with the Father and consecration to the Holy Spirit. Just as the entire Trinity effects the incarnation, with the result nonetheless that the human nature of Christ is rendered filial with respect to the Father and possessive and sending with respect to the Spirit, who also leads it—so humanity is modified in a threefold way by the indwelling Trinity. God's act of will is one. Its effect is threefold.

Perhaps Mersch's boldest piece of theological reasoning is one that in its basic assumption, not to speak of its development, would distress the East. Since the eternal Word is Spirator of the Spirit, says Mersch, the humanity of Christ which subsists in that Word partakes in the nature and relation of a Spirator. Therefore the baptized too come to have a part in breathing forth the Spirit, since they are fellow-men and brothers in a new way to him who is Spirator.

The chief difficulty attending this theological question is that the West has so consistently restricted the Trinity's activity to efficient causality in man's sanctification that nothing but a theory of appropriation of roles to the persons is left. St. Thomas has lent the weight of his authority to the view by omitting any relation of adoptive sonship by the Christian specifically to the Father. The Father is Father to the Son, but God in three persons has adoptive fatherhood over us, in his thinking.

We may not forget that this appropriation scheme is theological theory and not faith. The trend of most contemporary writing on the divine indwelling is in the direction of a *"proprium"* theory of some sort, namely, one that relates the soul in grace not simply to God as One but to God as Three.

The theory of quasi-formal causality has proved helpful to numerous modern trinitarian theologians. It maintains that the divine Three are not merely the efficient cause of man's holiness but serve as formal cause, as it were, of his knowledge and love of God both in grace and glory. If "created grace" is the term commonly used to describe that accidental quality or modification of the human spirit which follows (by nature, not temporally), upon the presence and activity of the divine Three, then "uncreated grace"—despite its drab and neutral sound—stands for the Three whose presence results in this modification. K. Rahner has cited the pertinent biblical texts and the theological monographs done both on them and on the writings of the Fathers on the divine indwelling. ("Some Implications of the Scholastic Concept of Uncreated Grace," *Theological Investigations,* 1, 319–24). These show conclusively that the scriptural and patristic emphasis was on the personal Spirit whom God sent to men, on Christ who abides in us, on God who shows mercy by communicating himself to justified men. In other words, the "uncreated gift" of the triune God himself to mankind is primary in human holiness. Every created grace, every way of man's being *pneumatikós* ("spirited," i.e.) is a consequence and a manifestation of the possession of this uncreated grace.

In scholastic theology the emphasis was shifted to created grace, the very converse of the initial stress, writes Rahner. "However diverse they may be among themselves, it is true of all the scholastic theories that they see God's indwelling and His conjunction with the justified man as based exclusively on created grace. In virtue of the fact that created grace is imparted to the soul, God imparts himself to it and dwells in it." (*Ibid.*, p. 324) Rahner points out that the scholastic emphasis does not vitiate the biblical-patristic, but may be seen as the more readily manageable expression of the same reality. After all, there is no priority *in time* of grace to divine indwelling or vice versa, only *in thought*. The new "relation" of God to man in the divine inhabitation can more readily be conceived of as founded on an absolute modification of man himself. God does not change in coming to man or sending his Son or Spirit upon him. The reality of grace is best explained, the scholastics held, in terms of that supernatural participation in God's nature through man's likeness-in-being to him in his spirituality and holiness. However created grace (i.e., the change in man) may be conceived—whether as the result of a new exercise of efficient causality by God, or as an elevation of man in all his powers giving him the potential capacity to possess God in beatific vision, or as a friendship which provides a new and sufficient basis for the presence of God in man, already there in fact—we must realize that in the scholastic view the indwelling of the Holy Spirit (and with him Father and Son) is a *consequence* of the bestowal of created grace. With the alteration of man by grace, man and God are in a new relation, and God is the end-term, so to say, of this relation.

The shift of emphasis back to the Three who dwell in us and thereby make us like them can be achieved only when it is seen who Father, Son, and Spirit are to us in grace and glory. They are not merely the efficient cause of our holiness, acting as one divine being. They are Three who individually are the ground of our knowledge and love once we apprehend them in faith. They take the place, in the beatific vision, of created *species* (the images of objects that modify man as knower, once he has focused his mind on them). The blessed one has a new self-consciousness of his modified status through being related to Father, Son, and Holy Spirit immediately and directly. The Three become as it were the "form" of his thoughts and will-acts: "as it were" (*quasi*-formal), to protect the transcendence of the infinite God, though in fact the whole being of the blessed is "in-formed" by the Three with whom he is in this relation. Note that more has happened to him than a change in him efficiently caused by the triune God. *By revelation it has been told us that Father, Son, and Spirit are to be related to us in a new way.* (Father: 1 Jn 4,4.12f.15; Son: Jn 6,56; 14,20; 1 Jn 3,24; Rom 8,10; Gal 2,20; Eph 3,17; Spirit: Jn 14,16f; 1 Jn 4,13; Rom 5,5; 8,9,11,15,23; 1 Cor 2,12). We argue to the fullness of this threefold relation in the realm of glory ("beatific vision") from what we have been told of it in the realm of grace (divine self-donation). The two are, ontologically, homogeneous, the one being the commencement in time of the other.

There is a unique case in the order of grace which is not to be confused under any circumstances with the condition of justified man in grace or glory. It is the situation of the incarnation in which the eternal Word ("uncreated act," in the terminology of M. de la Taille) produced a "created actuation" in the humanity of Jesus. Union of Father, Son, and Holy Ghost with a justified man does not comprise an immediate actuation of his essence, as in the hypostatic union of the Word with the human nature of Jesus Christ, but an actuation of the body-soul in its operations. The Christian knows the divine Three and loves them, individually and distinctly, because they who dwell in him are individual and distinct. By the communication of the divine life the Three who are one God impress on our souls a created, finite, analogous replica of themselves. The reality we call sanctifying grace is, therefore, as uncreated, a "miniature trinity" in the essence of our beings. This assimilation of the Three is accomplished by our knowing and loving them who have not only been revealed to us but who have come to us and taken up their abode with us.

Rahner points out how Lessius, Scheeben, and even Galtier—the champion of created grace as a work of divine efficient causality—are aware that God's Spirit is the author of a properly assimilative action. Going farther back, he adduces support for his thesis in Alexander of Hales, Bonaventure, and Aquinas, all of whom at one point or other teach created grace as a consequence of the Holy Spirit's action. He is the "inhering, formal cause" of our adoptive sonship for St. Thomas (*S.Th.*, 3ª,7,13), who writes elsewhere: "Divine persons in virtue of an imprint of themselves leave certain gifts in our souls, whereby we formally enjoy (God), in other words love and wisdom." (1 *Sent.*, dist. 14, g. 2, 2.1 sol. 2) Quite simply, Rahner maintains that certain nuances of the earlier medieval theologians escaped the later schoolmen.

The important thing to remember is that the question of a proper relation to the three divine persons in their personal distinction is an open one. It may not be flatly stated by way of objection to any *"proprium"* theory that the only way one divine person can be in relation to a creature in distinction from the other two is by way of hypostatic unity, such as is given in Christ's case alone. The reason that it may not be stated is that it is impossible to prove. There is the one case where the divine person, the Word, is communicated to a particular human nature precisely to be person to and in it. In all other cases, who is to say that all three divine persons may not communicate themselves so as to be quasi-formal causes of love and knowledge of Three as distinct?

> In Scripture it is the Father in the Trinity who is our Father, and not the threefold God. The Spirit dwells in us in a particular and proper way. These and like statements of Scripture are first of all 'in possession.' . . . We must take Scripture and the expressions it uses in as exact a sense as we possibly can . . . In the history of Western piety an attenuation of the 'Trinity of the economy of salvation' into a kind of pre-Christian monotheism (and that is what the doctrine of bare appropriations in the theology of grace really amounts to) has . . . diminished the significance of the Holy Trinity in concrete religious life . . . In Scripture the interior Trinity and the Trinity of the economy of salvation are seen and spoken of in themselves with such simultaneity that there would be no justification in itself (logically) for taking the expressions literally and substantially in the first case and only in an 'appropriated' way in the second. (Rahner, *ibid.*, pp. 345f)

All this modern theorizing, like the medieval, may give the appearance of a dull interchange of philosophical ideas. In fact its purpose is practical and immediate: to restore to Christians their full heritage of faith. Daniélou says that the world of existence, the real world that is, reveals itself to us as a universe of persons united by love. Love exists eternally in God in the Trinity of divine persons. The community of spirits in the world who are united by love is a manifestation of the divinity which is Three. Between the divine Trinity and the human community there exists a bond of love and of communication which is the person of Christ, true God and true man. "He is the cosmic tree reuniting what is below and what is on high, what is East and what is West, by the outreaching sign of his cross." (*The Scandal of Truth*, p. 69) The whole meaning of Christian life is the invitation extended to the family of man to have eternal intercommunion—intimate friendship—with the divine Three. We have not grasped the meaning of the gospel until we are clear on where matters will end if we accept it in faith and live it in charity.

"May they all be one," Jesus prayed, "as you, Father, are in me, and I in you, so also *may they be in us,* that the world may believe that you did send me. The glory which you gave me I have given to them, that they may be one as we are one; I in them and you in me, may they be perfectly one." (Jn 17,21ff)

Selected Readings

GENERAL

Franks, R. S., *The Doctrine of the Trinity* (London: Duckworth, 1953) [Includes a history of the doctrine in the Lutheran, reform, and antitrinitarian traditions].

Hodgson, L., *The Doctrine of the Trinity* (London: Nisbet, 1943).

Klein, F., *The Doctrine of the Trinity* (New York: Kenedy, 1940).

Michel, A., "Trinité," *Dictionnaire de théologie catholique*, 15² (Paris: Letouzey et Ané, 1950), cc. 1548–1855.

CHAPTER ONE

Knight, G. A. F., *A Biblical Approach to the Doctrine of the Trinity* (Edinburgh: Oliver & Boyd, 1953).

Lebreton, J., *History of the Dogma of the Trinity from Its Origins to the Council of Nicaea*, Vol. I, tr. Algar Thorold (London: Burns Oates & Washbourne, 1939); Vol. II, 8th ed. (Paris: G. Beauchesne, 1927).

Rahner, K., *Theological Investigations*, Vol. I (Baltimore: Helicon, 1961), pp. 79-148.

Stauffer, E., *New Testament Theology*, tr. John Marsh (New York: Macmillan, 1955).

Wainwright, A. W., *The Trinity in the New Testament* (London: Society for Promoting Christian Knowledge, 1962).

CHAPTER TWO

Bettenson, H., ed., *Documents of the Christian Church* (2d ed.; London: Oxford, 1963).

Daniélou, J., *Origen*, tr. Walter Mitchell (New York: Sheed & Ward, 1955).

————, "The God of Jesus Christ," *God and the Ways of Knowing* (New York: Meridian Books, 1960), pp. 139-73.

Kelly, J. N. D., *Early Christian Creeds* (London: Longmans, Green, 1950).

————, *Early Christian Doctrines* (London: Adam and Charles Black, 1958).

Prestige, G. L., *God in Patristic Thought* (London: Society for Promoting Christian Knowledge, 1952) [first pub. 1936].

Quasten, J., *Patrology*, Vols. II and III (Westminster, Md.: Newman, 1953/60).

CHAPTER THREE

Augustinus Aurelius, St., "On the Trinity," *Basic Writings of St. Augustine, II*, ed. Whitney J. Oates (New York: Random House, 1948), pp. 667-878.

Moriones, F., *Enchiridion Sancti Augustini* (Madrid: La Editorial Catolica, 1961), pp. 101-41.

Portalié, E., *A Guide to the Thought of St. Augustine,* tr. Ralph Bastian, with an introduction by Vernon J. Bourke (Chicago: Regnery, 1960). [This translation is from the article, "S. Augustin," which appeared in the *Dictionnaire de Théologie Catholique*].

CHAPTER FOUR

Anselm, St., *Basic Writings: Monologium; Proslogium; Gaunilon's "On behalf of the Fool"; Cur deus homo,* tr. S. W. Deane (La Salle, Ill.: Open Court Publishing Co., 1962).

Congar, Y. M-J., "God's . . . Dwelling among Men . . . under the Old and . . . New . . . Dispensation," Appendix III, *The Mystery of the Temple* (Baltimore: Helicon, 1962), pp. 262-99.

Gill, J., *The Council of Florence* (Cambridge: University Press, 1959).

Knowles, D., *The Evolution of Medieval Thought* (Baltimore: Helicon, 1962).

Meyendorff, J., *The Orthodox Church* (New York: Pantheon, 1962).

Smulders, P., *La doctrine trinitaire de S. Hilaire de Poitiers* (Rome: Gregorian University, 1944).

Thomas Aquinas, St., *Summa Theologica,* Vol. I, Part I, Questions 27-43, tr. English Dominican Fathers (New York: Benziger, 1947), pp. 147-226.
———, *Theological Texts,* sel. and tr., with notes by Thomas Gilby (London: Oxford, 1955).

Vaggaggini, C., "The Liturgy and the Christological and Trinitarian Dialectic of Salvation," *Theological Dimensions of the Liturgy,* I (Collegeville, Minn.: Liturgical Press, 1960), pp. 107-39.

CHAPTER FIVE

Mersch, E., "The Blessed Trinity," Book Four, *The Theology of the Mystical Body* (St. Louis: B. Herder, 1952), pp. 325-452.

Rahner, K., "Some Implications of the Scholastic Concept of Uncreated Grace," *Theological Investigations,* I (Baltimore: Helicon, 1961), pp. 319-46.

de Régnon, T., *Études de théologie positive sur la Sainte Trinité,* 4 vols. (Paris: 1892–98).

Scheeben, M. J., "The Mystery of the Most Holy Trinity," *The Mysteries of Christianity* (St. Louis: B. Herder, 1945), pp. 25-197.

Shea, W. M., and Wrenn, M. J., "The Relationship of the Christian to the Trinity," *The Dunwoodie Review,* I (January, 1961), 38-68; (April, 1961), 111-36.

ABBREVIATIONS

The Books of the Old and New Testaments

Genesis	Gn	Canticle of Canticles	Ct
Exodus	Ex	Wisdom	Wis
Leviticus	Lv	Sirach (Ecclesiasticus)	Sir
Numbers	Nm	Isaia	Is
Deuteronomy	Dt	Jeremia	Jer
Joshua	Jos	Lamentations	Lam
Judges	Jgs	Baruch	Bar
Ruth	Ru	Ezechiel	Ez
1 Samuel (1 Kings)	1 Sm	Daniel	Dn
2 Samuel (2 Kings)	2 Sm	Osea	Os
1 Kings (3 Kings)	1 Kgs	Joel	Jl
2 Kings (4 Kings)	2 Kgs	Amos	Am
1 Chronicles (Paralipomenon)	1 Chr	Abdia	Abd
2 Chronicles (Paralipomenon)	2 Chr	Jona	Jon
Ezra	Ez	Michea	Mi
Nehemia (2 Ezra)	Neh	Nahum	Na
Tobia	Tb	Habacuc	Hb
Judith	Jdt	Sophonia	So
Esther	Est	Aggai	Ag
Job	Jb	Zacharia	Za
Psalms	Ps(s)	Malachia	Mal
Proverbs	Prv	1 Machabees	1 Mc
Coheleth (Ecclesiastes)	Coh	2 Machabees	2 Mc

In the enumeration of the Psalms, the first number follows the Vulgate, the number within brackets, the Hebrew text.

St. Matthew	Mt	1 Timothy	1 Tim
St. Mark	Mk	2 Timothy	2 Tim
St. Luke	Lk	Titus	Ti
St. John	Jn	Philemon	Phlm
Acts of the Apostles	Ac	Hebrews	Heb
Romans	Rom	St. James	Jas
1 Corinthians	1 Cor	1 St. Peter	1 Pt
2 Corinthians	2 Cor	2 St. Peter	2 Pt
Galatians	Gal	1 St. John	1 Jn
Ephesians	Eph	2 St. John	2 Jn
Philippians	Phil	3 St. John	3 Jn
Colossians	Col	St. Jude	Jude
1 Thessalonians	1 Thes	Apocalypse	Ap
2 Thessalonians	2 Thes		

Apocrypha and Qumrân Material

Henoch	Hen	Testament of the	
Jubilees	Jub	Twelve Patriarchs	Test
Psalms of Solomon	Ps Sol	Manual of Discipline	MD

Other Source Material

Acta Apostolicae Sedis
   [Acts of the Apostolic See]   *AAS*
Ancient Christian Writers,
   ed. J. Quasten and others   *ACW*
Acta Sanctae Sedis
   [Acts of the Holy See]   *ASS*
Codex Iuris Canonici
   [Code of Canon Law]   *CIC*
Corpus Scriptorum Ecclesiasticorum
   Latinorum
   [Body of Latin Ecclesiastical
   Writings]   *CSEL*
Denzinger-Schönmetzer,
   Enchiridion Symbolorum, 32d ed.
   [Handbook of the Creeds]   D
Sacrorum Conciliorum nova
   . . . Collectio   *Mansi*
Patrologia, series graeca,
   ed. J. P. Migne   *PG*

Patrologia, series latina,
   ed. J. P. Migne   *PL*
Rouët de Journel, M. J.
   Enchiridion Patristicum, 21st ed.
   [Patristic Handbook]   R
Summa contra Gentes
   S. Thomae Aquinatis   *S.C.G.*
Quatuor Libri Sententiarum
   Petri Lombardi [Four Books
   of Opinions]   *Sent.*
Summa Theologiae
   S. Thomae Aquinatis   *S.Th.*
Supplementum tertiae partis Summae
   Theologiae (Ottawa ed. 1941)
                   Suppl.
The Church Teaches,
   ed. J. Clarkson and others   *TCT*

INDEX